C0-AZG-813

"The stories of your youth and your climb to success in Unlikely Journey are just fascinating. They are so realistic they make me feel as though I am actually there. What a mesmerizing journey reading it was. I really do like the way you have tied everything together with the overriding theme of "Choices." What a beautiful and inspiring gift for you to leave your grandchildren. You have given them guidance and help about the choices they will someday invariably have to make. It was truly a delight to read!"

-Sara Kidd

UNLIKELY
journey

Holly,
Hope you enjoy the
journey.

James A. Stilth
May 16, 2012

UNLIKELY
journey

JAMES H. STILTNER

BOOKLOGIX®

Alpharetta, Georgia

Copyright ©2012 by James H. Stiltner

All rights reserved. No part of this book may be reproduced or transmitted in any form or by any means, electronic or mechanical, including photocopying, recording, or any information storage and retrieval system, without permission in writing from James H. Stiltner.

ISBN: 978-1-61005-177-4

Library of Congress Control Number: 2012906467

Printed in the United States of America

∞This paper meets the requirements of ANSI/NISO Z39.48-1992 (Permanence of Paper)

Scripture taken from the HOLY BIBLE, NEW INTERNATIONAL VERSION®. Copyright ©1973.1978.1984 International Bible Society. Used by permission of Zondervan. All rights reserved.

The opinions and memories are those of the author, James H. Stiltner, to the best of his knowledge of events as they transpired. The following text contains recreated events, locations, and conversations from the author's memories of them.

I dedicate this book to my family.
Thank you for all of your support
and patience as the book unfolded.

Cordelia "Della" Stiltner

My Inspiration

The words of Robert Frost
provide some perspective to this endeavour:

"Two roads diverged in a wood, and I–

I took the one less travelled by,

And that has made all the difference."

"The Road Not Taken"
-Robert Frost

Breaks Interstate Park

TABLE OF CONTENTS

FOREWORD

This undertaking explores some of the experiences that affected me and those who shared my zeal to find out what was just beyond the next horizon. The earliest memories I had as a child were a mixed bag of daydreams, wishful thinking, and some honest-to-goodness dreams of what might be or what might still be waiting to happen. Early on, it was apparent that life would be different as we were able to observe the difficulties of growing older and interacting with the world around us. The daydreams faded away and the wishful thinking gave way to the realities of more difficult decisions that helped to fashion our destiny. The real dreams provided incentive for our journey through life as we sought to discover what lay beyond the horizon. Is the unreachable star really that inaccessible? Is the impossible dream worthy of consideration as a light in the forest or a beacon to guide us through the valleys to the mountain tops just over the horizon?

Young men dream dreams and old men remember what might have been. Choices that change people and the consequences of those choices are the substance of man. An individual has experiences that mold and shape him throughout life. Most choices are not spectacular and one hardly notices that lives are shaped with little fanfare. Man is the sum total of all his experiences along with consequences which occur because of decisions he makes or the decisions that are made for him. It is the experiences that are out of the ordinary which draw attention and may even provide encouragement to dream dreams and prompt one to reach for the stars. This undertaking explores some of my life experiences and how they affected me and those who shared my Don Quixotic-like journey through life.

It is in this context that these short stories or vignettes are offered to friends, families, and interested individuals to help them understand why certain decisions or choices were made and how the consequences of the actions changed lives.

PREFACE

G od created man and gave him the freedom to choose between right and wrong. What a powerful position for a mere mortal to possess. For the most part, he controls his own destiny. Life has many twists and turns which call for responses and reactions to virtually everything that is said or done. How many times has a decision been made only to regret the choice later? It is not uncommon to second guess and ask the question, "What if I had accepted the other alternative or chosen the path most travelled?"

There will be many opportunities to be confronted with a choice of which path to follow, which direction to take, and whose council to seek. An individual may choose to make the decision or to defer to others and allow life to "just happen." Relinquishing too many opportunities may jeopardize any chance to exercise some control over their destiny. There are consequences to every decision that will affect one or more people. Those effects will be positive or negative and result in changes that, in some cases, will be helpful and harmful in others.

Control over one's destiny is limited. We are aware that some things never change, so complete control is not possible. Newton's laws of motion, for instance, state that for every action in the universe there is an equal and opposite reaction. Another states that an object at rest will remain at rest until acted on by an outside force. Man must work within these parameters and accept them as constants and work to improve those which can be changed.

Choices come with responsibilities. The consequences of a decision to pursue a particular path may be insignificant or it can be life changing. The choice may be as simple as deciding whether to have steak or chicken for dinner. It can also be as serious as deciding whether or not to say yes to a marriage proposal. The choice may be to pick the lesser of two evils, or the vote may be to do nothing. However, to do nothing is still making a choice and there will be consequences. One's vote should not be relinquished too easily.

ACKNOWLEDGMENTS

I am most appreciative for all the help and support of the people who made it possible for this document to be completed. First and foremost, it was a privilege to have an opportunity to interact with individuals who stood shoulder to shoulder to assist when difficult issues and problems had to be faced. Whether simple or complex, the support of colleagues, friends, and family was especially evident when the path less travelled had to be considered.

Secondly, those who rallied to the call to lend assistance without hesitation were indispensable. I am grateful to all who helped to keep me focused to the task. Their criticism and suggestions were of immense value to keep content and presentation to a reasonable, believable and interesting level.

I would also like to thank Ahmad Meradji, Jessica Parker, Sara Strish, Caroline Donahue, and the entire BookLogix staff for helping me to keep my head on straight while publishing this book.

I take full responsibility for the idioms collected over the years.

Dad, Patricia, and Jim

Patricia, Ruby, and Peggy

First Family of SACS Secondary Commission

Wayne Shortridge Family: Wayne, Georgia, Phyllis,
Jeannie, Betty, Lois, Millie, and Keaster

INTRODUCTION

P rior to 1994, the families of Kenneth Kidd, James Stiltner, Jerome Schall, and Wayne Shortridge were unaware of the existence of each other. Kenneth and Sara lived with their children, Mary Helon (Molly) and Russell, in Dalton, Georgia. Ken and Sara were teachers and are now retired from the Dalton City Schools and they live in the community of Resaca which is near the city of Dalton. Molly graduated from the University of Georgia in Athens and followed in the footsteps of her parents to become a teacher and school administrator. Russell is pursuing a degree from Kennesaw State University and aspires to become a counselor.

The Schall family lives in Sarasota, Florida where the father, Jerome is employed by the city and the mother, Jacqueline Bishop MacDougall, is the office manager for an orthopedic dental office. There are three daughters, Jill Miller who is in obstetrics, Jaymi Delcos who is a police officer and Jeana who graduated from Florida State University and eventually found her way to Atlanta and currently works for an organization called Lexus Nexus.

The Wayne Shortridge family is a prominent and respected part of the community of Grundy, Virginia and their presence can be traced back to the early settlement of that part of Virginia. Wayne and Georgia had six children, Keaster, Jeanie, and Lois, twins Betty and Phyllis, and Mildred. They made a living in the coal business, but as the children matured they moved away to other parts of the country. Wayne and Georgia lived out their lives in Buchanan County.

The James Stiltner family migrated to Atlanta by way of Richmond, Virginia. Jim and Phyllis and their sons, Christopher (Chris) and Brian lived in Dunwoody, Georgia, but relocated to Cumming, Georgia in 1995. Phyllis is a retired Business Education Teacher and Jim retired from the Southern Association of Colleges and Schools in December of 2001. Chris, the younger son, graduated from the University of Georgia and elected to pursue a different direction for his life by choosing to seek his fortune in the business world. He works for a company called Peak Ten. Brian spent two years at the University of Georgia before transferring to Georgia State University in Atlanta where he graduated and eventually became a school administrator.

These families could just have easily been like ships passing in the night, but fate would have it otherwise. Brian and Molly were the first to arrive at a crossroads and be faced with a decision that dramatically changed the lives of many people. They were the catalysts that brought the families together. Their decision to be married on March 2, 1996, forged a bond of friendship and kinship for the families that grew over the years and provided an extended family environment. The circle increased when Molly and Brian gave birth to Nathan James on December 31, 1999, to be followed soon after by Sara Elizabeth on October 14, 2002.

The Schall family entered the circle when Chris and Jeana married on December 29, 2005. Their addition to the family was Jackson Allen. It appeared that equilibrium had been reached, but there is always room for one more. Jeana, Chris, and Jackson loaded the car and drove to the hospital on Sunday July 26, 2009, and welcomed an addition to the family. A beautiful blue-eyed blond named Reese Adriane was born at 8:15 a.m. and the family circle would never be the same.

The ever widening family circle provided opportunities to meet and celebrate life. The activities grew exponentially as the grandparents were introduced again to the world of soccer, basketball, baseball, softball, dance, and karate, with football, golf, and cheerleading waiting in the wings. Add events such as birthdays, Christmas, Thanksgiving, anniversaries, and any number of such occasions and the families that were once unaware of each other are now part of an expanding family circle.

Special events are important because they allow families to keep in touch, not to mention the opportunity to enjoy good food, fun, fellowship, and conversation. Topics of conversation at these functions usually run the gamut from politics, to education, to world affairs, and especially the grandchildren. It is a known fact that the grandchildren are no doubt the smartest, most talented, most handsome, most beautiful to be found anywhere. A bit prejudiced, you say? Well maybe, but isn't that the way it is supposed to be?

One such occasion, probably someone's birthday, found the group relating some of the experiences that had affected them and the consequences that resulted in changed lives. The discussion on this particular day also included speculation about how life would have been different had the path not chosen been chosen. How would life have been changed if I had chosen to enter the Aviation Officer Cadet Training Program to become a Navy jet pilot rather than become an educator? What if Ken and Sara had never settled in Dalton and Molly and Brian did, in fact, pass like strangers in the night? What if Chris had chosen to go to Georgia Tech and Jeana had chosen to become a Florida Gator? However, the choices that were made either by them or for them, with apologies to Robert Frost, made all the difference.

The discussion on this day was so spirited and lively that someone suggested it might be interesting and beneficial to record some of the experiences that had changed lives. The children and future generations might be interested to know something about their roots and how their lives had changed as a result of decisions or choices that had been made even before some of them were born.

It might also make them aware of undesirable consequences of certain actions which could be avoided rather than have history repeat itself. It might also provide encouragement to future generations to strive for excellence if they see that others have been successful. A goal or goals thought to be unachievable may be very reachable as evidenced by the experiences of someone within the expanded family. The consequences of a poor decision in the past may not be so destructive and even avoided if there was a record of what occurred in a similar situation in the past. Lessons learned or not learned can change a life forever.

Good idea, but who should write the document? Ken and Sara were enthusiastic about having me undertake the task of using my experiences and decisions to illustrate how they had affected my life and the lives of those people with whom I had interacted.

Problems and their solutions had common elements, but ultimately, the work would have to take on the characteristics of an autobiography. Accepting the responsibility for the task was a challenge to my writing ability, but Sara and Ken were convinced that I should write the document and the die was cast.

No attempt will be made to present a full-blown history of the extended family; and, the finished product, if it is ever finished, will be subject to the limitations of my observations and the interpretation of events as I encountered them. Glimpses of my soul may be laid open for all to see in some instances, as a result of my actions or inactions. One is judged more critically by history sometimes for what they did not do than by what they did do. The choice of a title for this work was selected to document events that occurred and changed lives, and also to emphasize the importance of reaching to achieve that which may appear to be unreachable. A series of vignettes or short stories will be documented to show how the decisions that were made did, in fact, alter lives over a number of decades.

These vignettes, or short stories, contain descriptions of major events (and some not so major), which held some surprises that could have been predicted and others that changed the direction of my life. These short stories contain considerable background information that will be referred to throughout this document. Hopefully, these short stories, some portrayed in a light vein and others in a more serious tone, will be interesting and informative and provide a glimpse of life as it changed for one individual and how that one life influenced decisions that affected thousands of people. The influence of an individual from the coal mining region of Appalachia was so unlikely that one would see it as a sojourn to be experienced only through dreams. However, it reached from the coal mining region of Virginia to the palatial environs of the heads of state in many countries.

The stories are based on fact and references are used to emphasize a point rather than to develop or defend a hypothesis. The only primary source of information offered is the selective memories of events in my life and how they affected and changed lives. The style of writing is strictly that of the author and may or may not be correct or "according to Hoyle." This project is not intended to focus on my accomplishments, but rather to record and give credit to those who made it possible for good things to happen.

Prior to launching into the world of literary excellence, there are certain disclaimers that must be established. The purpose of this undertaking is not to suggest that there is only one right answer or that there is only one right choice, but to provide evidence that with enough determination and effort and a little help from friends and colleagues almost any goal is achievable. A Chinese proverb states, "A great journey begins with a single step." That first, single step is crucial for it may well decide the future.

No attempt has been made to offer this work as an autobiography and the vignettes may not be presented in chronological order. Hopefully, it will chronicle events and experiences that have had profound influence on me and those individuals around me. It may also give some insight into my personality and character and may indicate prejudices unknown to me. Time and space do not permit a thorough coverage of life as it was and is, and the consensus of opinion was that the events and experiences contained herein are unique enough to warrant making a record of them for posterity.

The sequence of events and the precise timing described in some of the vignettes may appear a bit far-fetched. They are true to the extent that selective memory allows one to believe so deeply that some of the events sounded so good that they just had to be true. Everything I said was true, but some were truer than others. Cross my heart and hope to die if it is not true.

Events happened that suggest the possibility of divine intervention. There is no doubt, in the opinion of the writer, that a higher power was directing the footsteps of individuals in many instances. That higher power was God working in and through lives. Whether it is a case of cause and effect, action and reaction, or divine intervention, one can be confident that God is in control and the prayer is for the good sense to recognize that fact and accept it. Future generations will be able to relate to some of these experiences and possibly profit from them. It is with this sense of inadequacy that I accept the responsibility to take pen in hand to write down those experiences and decisions that affected the lives of many people.

Here is where it all began in the beautiful high school built by the Works Progress Administration (WPA). The building has been renovated and is now the Appalachian School of Law.

Grundy High School

PART ONE

At Home in Grundy

Old Grundy

WHAT IS IN A NAME?

A good name is worthy of praise and should be protected at all costs. The choice for a name can be one of the most important events in a person's life. While one has little input into the name by which they are to be called, it is important to know that they will likely have the name for as long as they live. A newborn is like a blank sheet of paper. The youngster develops mentally and physically, experiences life, and begins to collect those characteristics that will define him as an individual. Just as a blank paper is identified by the characters recorded thereon, a name is recognized by those qualities with which it is associated.

Has the retort, "His reputation precedes him," ever been used to describe someone you know? A name can be identified with traits like honesty, trustworthiness, and truthfulness. A name with a good reputation was very important in the times of early settlement. At that time, a name was the test of a man and everything was judged off the reputation associated with that name. It had to be protected against theft because anyone could steal a name at that time. Therefore, it had to be guarded to insure that it could be trusted. Many transactions were sealed with a handshake. Paranoia reigned when names could not be trusted; no one wanted an untested name to be associated with their close-knit circle. Maintaining a good name and reputation went far to enhance attempts to be successful. It was difficult to make headway if a name was not well known, but to establish oneself without a name at all was near impossible.

By today's standards, most of the early settlers in the southwestern part of Virginia were poor. It took a special breed of people to settle this mountainous area where the borders of Virginia joined West Virginia and Kentucky. The area was described in a book written by Sam Hurley and Judge Willis Staton. They noted:

> These mountains seem to tower a little higher, and from their rugged sides of the cliffs appear to overhang a little farther than all the others. The growth of forest is dense, the valleys deeper, the shadows linger longer, and are of a darker hue. This

section is more remote and inaccessible than any other portion of the Appalachian range...The first white men who hazarded their lives by penetrating these mountain heights, stood by the river [most likely the Levisa], and most appropriately christened it DISMAL. No other word could have so completely characterized the entire region.[1]

An amusing incident grew out of frequent interchanges between residents of the area and visitors asking for directions. Visitors would ask about the area, whereupon residents responded, "This is Dismal." Their retort was always, "I didn't ask for the condition of the surrounding area. I want to know the name of this place." Perplexed, residents would reply, "It is a depressing place and its name is Dismal."

Oh, but the stories that grew out of that lonely stretch of U.S. Route 460. What was dismal for some was wild and wonderful to others.

Establishing a name and building a reputation was very important in the rapidly growing area that came to be known as Buchanan County. Having been fortunate enough to gain a foothold in this area, the Stiltner name was recognized and accepted by the residents of the community.

---

[1] Sam Hurley, and Judge Willis Staton, *A Colorful Career of a Miraculous Mountaineer: A Glimpse into the Life of a Remarkable Character*, (Pikeville, KY: 1943), 70.

Somewhere in time the name Stiltner was established and therein is the basis of a story that is bittersweet but never dull. Oral history or legend, probably the latter, has it recorded that Lawson Kelly Stiltner and Cordelia Keen (her family knew her as Della) had a stormy courtship. As the story goes, Lawson was quite a ladies' man and cherished his freedom. Love found a way and the gentile and beautiful young lady from Meeting House Branch convinced the rambunctious young man from Stiltner's Creek that he could search the world over and not find a better mate. Reluctantly, John Arthur Keen and Mahalia Davis Keen gave the hand of their daughter, Cordelia, in marriage to Lawson Kelly Stiltner, son of William Cecil and Hettie Stiltner.

The James Stiltner family was difficult to trace and could have been lost in the confusion. My grandfather was orphaned early in his life and was raised by a family named Dales. It was the family of Preston Dales that kept him for their own for much of his young life, prompting many people to refer to him as Cecil Dales, even though he was always a Stiltner. When he was old enough, William Cecil Stiltner left his adoptive family and struck out on his own.

There was one thing that was unmistakable about Grandpa Stiltner. He was the epitome of a mountain man. He raised his family on one hundred acres of land that belonged to absentee land owner, J .G. Bustion. Mr. Bustion made a pact with Cecil whereby he would allow the family to live on the land as long as they lived and would be caretakers of the property. The agreement was sealed with a handshake.

It is interesting to note that when Grandmother Stiltner died she was followed in death by Grandpa Stiltner one month later. He was burned to death in the old house that had been home for the family all their lives. It was as if the last page of a book had been turned and no evidence remained to indicate there had even been anyone who had lived in that place. In a few years, the growth of bushes and trees made it virtually impossible to pinpoint the exact spot where the old house had stood for so many years.

December 18, 1934, was a cold day when the Stiltner/ Keen legacy first saw the light of day; the first grandchild was born, and that child was me. It is ironic that the event was at a time when people were wondering whether or not they could survive the economic disaster called the Great Depression. It certainly was not a time to start a family.

Nevertheless, the right to choose a course of action was exercised and the child was born, but definitely without a silver spoon in his mouth. What name would be given to the blond, blue-eyed offspring of a coal miner and a stay-at-home mom? A baby inherits the family name, which comes with considerable baggage both good and bad. It may have to live up to a name that has a great legacy or it may have to live down a name with a bad reputation. Since the name rarely changes, whatever is associated with it is difficult to erase. Every effort should be taken to protect the name.

It is significant to point out that at this time in history men were expected to work and provide for the family and the wife stayed home and raised the children. The father worked hard and was away from home for much of the daylight hours. He loved his family, but was not one to make public display of his emotions. Naming the infant was probably considered to be woman's work.

Mother was just the opposite. She too loved her family, but was not hesitant to show her love and affection. Her choice for a name for her first born was unusual, and there was some concern and confusion that followed me for a lifetime. Her high expectations and aspirations were reflected in the choice and it prompted the selection of two first names after two kings, King James of England and King Harold from Sweden. If her son was to have an opportunity for greatness, she reasoned, he should have a name that commanded respect.

She also knew that a good name and reputation were very important to survive in the mountainous area of the state of Virginia. A man's word was sacred and many a deal was sealed with a handshake. Life was difficult, to say the least, and survival often depended upon whether or not one could trust his neighbor to tell the truth. A man was as good as his word and the word was his name.

The Great Depression brought hardship to everyone and Lawson's family was no exception. It was especially difficult for the poor. They had little to start with and even less as the country worked itself out of the depression. Life was harsh for most everyone who settled in the sparsely populated Appalachian Mountain area. Prosperity would eventually come to the region in the form of "black gold;" better known as coal. Coal mining replaced the lumbering industry and the economy of the area was raised as the rich resources of coal appeared to be unlimited. Some people became rich, others raised their standard of living, but the majority of the people were still victims of hard times. I was a child of the Great Depression and not old enough to understand what it meant when my parents talked about, "hard times."

Prior to attending school, there was not a problem. I had two perfectly good names and would be known as Harold to all my family. Elementary school was another story. I was in class with another boy whose name was Harold Stiltner. The teacher decided that two boys with the same name would be too confusing in the two room school and since the other boy had no middle name she announced that the one with two first names would be called James Harold. It was a name that I answered to for some people for the rest of my life. I was still Harold to the family, but now must answer to two names.

An interesting play on the name occurred in high school. Coaches have a unique way of identifying their athletes. Frank Spraker, the football coach, · preferred the name Jimmie Harold when calling on my questionable prowess as a wing back on the Grundy High School football team. The name caught on especially after an incident on the school grounds. My very first date was with a pretty young lady; we planned to go to the movies on Saturday at the Lynwood Theater. After enjoying the movie, sharing some popcorn and a Coca-Cola, we found our way to the swings on the school grounds. The young lady wanted to swing so I obliged. She urged me to, "Swing me higher Jimmie

Harold." She probably had heard the coach use the name and chose to use it also.

Wouldn't you just know that at that precise moment some of my football teammates walked by the swings. I was surprised when they passed by without saying a word. The silence did not last long. The next Monday afternoon when the football practice began, it was an open chorus of, "Swing me higher Jimmie Harold," each time my number was called. The heckling lasted through practice and beyond and the name Jimmie Harold was to follow me well into adult life.

The confusion continued in college. "What's His Name" was two weeks late in enrolling in college and the first day in class provided another name to be added to the growing list of how I was called. The math professor looked at his class roll and found the name of his newest student to be much too long. Without much ado he indicated the name, James Harold Stiltner, was too long and announced to the class that Jim was joining the class. Who was going to question the math professor on the first day of class for a student who was two weeks late to class?

How many names should a person have to answer to? To one group of people I was known as James, to others it was James Harold, to others I was Jimmie Harold. I was still called Harold by my immediate family and Buddy by my sisters. Later I was dubbed Doc by my future father-in-law. I juggled names, but tried to answer appropriately to all who called. As one could imagine, there was more than a little confusion and it prompted my wife-to-be to request she be informed when I decided on the name by which I wanted to be called. A name that started out with much promise was complicated beyond what it should have been. There is a point to this much ado about nothing. The name Jim finally sifted out and most everyone knows me by that name. At least, when someone calls on the telephone and asks for James Harold, Jimmie Harold, or Harold I know the party who is calling is someone from my past. "What is my name? My name–José Jiménez." Only the most mature friends and colleagues will relate to this question. The point is to know yourself and keep your name above reproach.

NEW NAME, NEW BEGINNING

The Stiltner name was established and there was never a dull moment. Oral history or legend, probably the latter, has it recorded that Lawson Kelly Stiltner and Cordelia Keen would be key players in establishing the Stiltner/Keen legacy. The families could not have been more different. The early 1800's was where the trail ends abruptly, but stories abound concerning the origin of the name Stiltner and perhaps it is sufficient to say that the name was chosen to escape a suspicious past. The fact that a man of German background could have been a deserter from the Hessian army and did not want to be found was a definite possibility.

Had he been conscripted into the army and sent to the remote area as a part of an exploratory mission? It is possible that he had left the army and fled into the area that became known as Buchanan County, Virginia. It was a rugged mountainous part of Virginia that provided ample hiding places to someone who did not want to be found. It is quite possible to postulate that our "hero" changed his name to Stiltner to avoid detection. It probably was not the first nor the last time someone would flee to this remote area to avoid detection. It is interesting to speculate on the facts that are known and construct a link to the past that would solve the mystery of the origin of the Stiltner family.

The name became a household word as the "new" residents became very prolific. It was so prolific that at a future date, my father-in-law-to-be, Wayne Shortridge, was moved to declare that there were more Stiltners in Buchanan County than there were stickweeds. Stickweeds are almost as plentiful as kudzu, but not quite. Those who are familiar with kudzu know it is a prolific plant, and to compare it with the rapidly growing Germanic settlers was not a bad analogy. It is a good bet that the name originated in that part of the country and it is also safe to assume that people located in other parts of the country originated from that same questionable lineage.

Regardless of family background, William Cecil Stiltner struck the deal of a lifetime with J. G. Bustion, guaranteeing them a home for life as long as they took care of the land. Sealed with a handshake, they lived out their lives on that property.

Cecil ruled with an iron hand and no one who valued his life dared trespass on the property. He and Hettie Angeline, everyone called her "Ma Hettie," did their part to keep the Stiltner name alive. They had six boys, David, George, Charlie, Kermit, Burns, and Lawson, but only three sons were fathered from them to keep the legacy alive. The three were Charlie's son Leo, Burns' son Billy, and me. We have passed that responsibility of keeping the name alive to my sons, Brian and Chris, Billy's son Stephen, and Leo's son Aaron. They, in turn, will leave Nathan James, Jackson Allen, and Aaron's son to keep the Stiltner family tree from expiring. That is not to say there were no females, but the women all married and assumed their husbands last name.

Patriarch Cecil and his family lived in an old house that probably never experienced any home improvements unless it was to stop a leak in the roof or fill a crack in the wall. He never owned a car, never had a job other than farming the land, never travelled more than forty miles from home, never met a quart of moonshine he didn't like, and never had to worry about income tax.

Earliest memories of Grandfather Stiltner were that he was always dressed in a long sleeved shirt and coveralls. He was never known to wear a short sleeved shirt. His abundant silver grey hair protruded from under an old felt hat that was removed only at meal times and at night. He always washed his hands and combed his hair before eating and if anyone sitting at his table did not do likewise, they could not eat. His beard and his hair grew intertwined so one was not certain where the beard began and the hair left off. One thing was a certainty, combing the hair and washing the face before eating was a ritual that was popular even before hand wash solution became available.

Grandfather Stiltner was a legend in his time. He was not afraid of man or beast. His fearless nature caused men of greater strength and will to give him a wide berth. An incident concerning a day in the dense woods to hunt for ginseng was classic "Pa Ceece." He was walking in some heavy brush that was about waist high when he felt something caught on the leg of his heavy overalls. Thinking it was a branch or briar, he walked until he could see his feet. He looked down to see what was clinging to his pant leg and lo and behold it was a copperhead snake. When asked what he did he replied, "I raised my leg and killed the snake with my trusty walking stick." He extricated himself from the snake's fangs and continued his trek through the woods. The poor snake just tangled with the wrong man.

The one modern convenience allowed in the house was a radio, which was turned on for the "Lum and Abner Show" and the news. The only other time the radio was turned on was to hear the Grand Ole Opry on Saturday night. Noise of any kind was not allowed while these programs were being aired. One particular topic of radio news was the disposition of the war. Everyone was concerned about the advance of the Red Army. Just what was a red army? I was too young to understand that they were talking about the Russian army. The news report was concerning the advance of the Russian army to the front lines where the Russians and the German army were engaged in battle that also included the U.S. troops since they were allies.

The family was much interested in the progress of the war because Uncle Arvil and Uncle Kermit were in the battle. Both came back alive, but Uncle Kermit was near to an exploding grenade that sent him scurrying to find a table or something to crawl under when he heard a loud noise. He never got over the incident the rest of his life.

The house full of boys could be loud at times, but they knew better than to interrupt when the radio was playing. The other time when silence was golden was story time. Pa Ceece could not read, but Ma Hettie could bring the pages of a western novel to life to the point where one felt totally involved. It is one of those treasured memories to be cherished forever. The family was a rowdy group to say the least. There was nothing refined about them, but they enjoyed life and were carefree and uninhibited. They were not above settling arguments with a scuffle or even a good old "knock down and drag out fight." Time spent with them was strictly in a male dominated environment and it definitely had an effect on anyone who grew up in it.

Residing no more than eight to ten miles from the rambunctious Stiltner clan, was the Keen family. There were six girls and two boys to help with the chores. It was very much the opposite of the swashbuckling youngsters of the male dominated Stiltner family. Della was one of six girls, Ellen, Stella, Jenny, Sarah, and Alta and they had two brothers, Milton and Johnny. Grandfather Keen, affectionately called "Poppy," was a tall, gruff looking man who was not at all gruff. Instead, he was one of the kindest men one would hope to meet. Early in life he worked for a lumbering company that cut large trees and floated them down the Levisa River to a gathering area where they could be sawed into lumber for distribution all over the country. His later life was concentrated on farming the land on which they lived. He, like Cecil, did not own the land and house in which they lived, but they paid rent or something in kind. Dan Clevenger and his family owned the land and were very benevolent when times were bad and there was not enough money to pay the rent. The family was able to stay in the old house until they all grew up and moved away or died.

The Keen family was of Scotch/Irish descent and had a kind and gentle demeanor. Grandmother Mahalia Davis Keen, everyone called her "Granny," was a diminutive figure, but she was a ball of energy. She never raised her voice when someone was misbehaving, but when she spoke everyone listened and minded their manners. Keeping harmony among six girls and two boys was a major task that she managed efficiently.

By today's standards most of the early settlers in the southwestern part of Virginia were poor. It took a special breed to settle in this rugged mountainous area where the borders of West Virginia and Kentucky came together with Virginia. The tri-state area was not only beautiful, but also rich in the history of feuding families like the Hatfields and McCoys. Harlin County, Kentucky, was a place that one did not want to be caught passing the time of day after five o'clock in the evening. It maintains the reputation as a place where one would not want to plan a vacation.

It is ironic to note that as this work is being edited for publication, a tragic event in this little known area of

Buchanan County was the scene for yet another blow to the Stiltner family. Uncle Burns was my favorite uncle and the news was splashed over the media that on Sunday, March 13, 2011, a shootout occurred between law enforcement and a would-be robber. Two officers were wounded and two were killed. One of the two officers who lost his life in the line of duty was William Ezra Stiltner. If there is any consolation, it is that Burns died three years before and did not have to mourn the tragic death of his only son.

THE BOUGH BENT BUT NEVER BROKE

T he early settlers toiled long and hard to extract a living from the land, and there was disagreement about the harsh reality of living there. Some felt living in the mountainous region instilled a sense of claustrophobia, but I and many others felt the mountains embraced our town, our own little part of the world. It was and is a beautiful part of the westernmost expanse of Virginia. Even though it was difficult to carve out a living in this wild and wonderful part of God's creation, the people who lived there were fiercely protective of what they had accomplished. The unparalleled beauty of that area cannot be disputed as evidenced by standing atop Lookout Mountain, Tennessee, where one can see eight states. However, some felt the lush vegetation caused a feeling of claustrophobia while others felt as if the mountains were a security blanket for them.

The settlers lived off the land by cultivating vegetable gardens, raising fields of grain, corn, and potatoes, grinding their flour and meal, and raising livestock for milk and meat. Doctors were few and far between so home remedies were important to them. They were self- sufficient and industrious and they utilized experience and local knowledge to stay healthy and safe.

"Signs" were very important. If the signs were not right, then don't plant the potatoes. This local knowledge was not always failsafe, but if decisions had to be rendered, it was always good to rely on what parents and grandparents taught. Such jewels of local knowledge like, "where you find one copperhead snake there will be another one nearby" or "an extra ring on a wooly worm means a hard winter is coming" are examples of the colorful explanations offered by the mountaineers. These were the signs we were taught and believed wholly in. Although we believed signs explained why certain things happened, no sign explained why the women had to work hard to prepare a large midday meal on Sunday, even though no work was to be done on the "Lord's Day."

Ginseng and yellow root were popular remedies that were used to treat a number of ailments. Ginseng was a particularly interesting herb. It grew in the mountains and its value was enhanced when the root, which was the part of the plant that was important, resembled the human torso. It grew in the wild and was sought after for its monetary value as well as its medicinal value.

It was not unusual for people to go "hunting" and search for the ginseng as a second objective. The question, "Where are you going?" could easily be answered with, "Goin' sangin'." The retort was not slang for singing, but had evolved from old English and was interpreted to mean one was searching for ginseng. The yellow root came from a tough briar and tasted so bitter that it could have easily been the origin of the phrase, "The cure is worse than the illness." It was supposed to cure any ailments of the stomach among other maladies.

Some of the "truisms" were helpful, but some of them may have been detrimental to a healthy existence. Blowing tobacco smoke into the ear was supposed to cure the earache. One interesting caution was never to drink sweet milk and eat fish at the same time. It was a caution that was never understood, but sweet milk and fish consumed together was definitely not recommended.

Children were expected to mind their table manners and the men were to be served first. Women and children ate after the men were finished, which meant there was the possibility that only the wings and backs were left, but the women did the cooking and there was plenty to go around. If worse came to worse, someone would chase down a chicken and put it in the pot.

Sundays were the occasions when large numbers of people gathered to eat. Grandmother Keen was famous for her chicken and dumplings, and it was not uncommon to have ten or twelve people drop by just to say hello. Their greetings were returned and all who came to visit were invited to sit and dine with them. Everyone knew the saying, "We were just passing by and thought we would stop and say hello." No one just said hello and left because everyone knew they would be invited to stay and sup with the family.

Like the popular ad for camel cigarettes, "I'd walk a mile for a Camel," friends and neighbors were eager to walk two miles for Haley's chicken and dumplings. It was not considered a burden, and more food was prepared for just such an occasion. That is unlike today when dropping by unexpectedly would be a huge breach of "proper" protocol.

Children were not to speak unless spoken to and were taught never to embarrass other people. It was always, "please pass the biscuits," and taking more than one at a time drew a sharp look from grandpa or grandma. Children were cautioned to eat what they wanted, but to take no more than they could eat. Food left on the plate could mean a lengthy stay at the table, a stomach ache, or both. Lessons were difficult at times, but much was learned by observing and listening to parents and grandparents. The warm and friendly environment was a learning venue, and children were hardly aware that they were absorbing values and knowledge to prepare them to be all they could be.

Now what does one do with a house full of young rambunctious boys? He puts them to work for one thing. Most people are knowledgeable of the term, "plowing new ground." The land was tillable, but was a challenge to prepare for planting crops. Plowing new ground was backbreaking work and after working all day cutting trees, removing rocks, stumps and other debris, the young men were ready for bed. They worked from sunup to sundown, six days a week. However, the Lord rested on the seventh day, and no one worked on Sunday. So life was not all bad. It didn't hurt that there was a family with six girls living no more than eight miles away.

Life was harsh for most everyone who settled in the Appalachian Mountain area. The area of the state was rich in coal and was an attraction for people seeking work. It was hard work and dangerous as well. The town of Grundy was a bustling mecca for people searching for good wages and it became the county seat. Despite the danger, men were attracted by the good wages and in its heyday, Grundy and the surrounding area was like a boom town. It would not remain such a prosperous place as the seams of coal played out and became more difficult and more expensive to extract from the earth.

The influence that shaped my early life was certainly diverse, and coal mining was a way of life in the mountains of Virginia. It was tempered by a mother's kind and gentle nature that helped to break the bonds that had held generations of families' captive by the coal industry. When asked why they chose to work in the mines the response was: their dad was a miner, his dad was a miner, and his grandfather and his father before him were miners. So what else is new?

Although the time I had to spend with my mother was painfully short, she was extremely influential in my life. She was a tower of strength and she instilled within me the value of having concern and respect for people and property, love of family, and most of all a love and respect of God. That influence included her deep concern that her son have the opportunity to "make something of your life" as it was often expressed.

DREAMS AND HOPES FOR THE FUTURE

My mother, Della, was the glue that held the family together and her teaching was through example. She had a hard life, but never complained when faced with problems both large and small. No one ever remembered hearing her talk about other people, but I did remember the lesson I learned about respecting other people. I was reprimanded for making fun of a man called "Tater Jake." The man walked the railroad tracks and happened to be passing by where we were playing. She heard us making fun of the old man and was quick to put a stop to the heckling. She reminded us that, "except for the grace of God, there go I." We were properly admonished and were careful not to be disrespectful again, especially to people less fortunate. She pointed out that all people were the same in God's eyes.

There was occasion to interact with Tater Jake in a more intimate way soon after the hazing incident. He was a strange man who walked along the tracks of the Norfolk and Western Railroad which passed within ten yards of our house. He would appear periodically and just as quickly disappear. No one knew where he came from and no one knew where he went. His strange behavior made him a target for ridicule, but there was some degree of respect for this man of mystery. Mother wanted me to find a way to apologize for his behavior and probably had something to do with what happened next.

I had three or four warts on the back of my hand and had been told that they were caused by frogs peeing on my hand. Mother didn't think for a moment that Tater Jake had mystical powers, but she went along with Dad when he suggested that they keep a watch by the railroad tracks until the old man returned. They waited and watched for the opportunity to talk with the man and when he did appear, I was apprehensive and approached him cautiously. A tentative hello elicited no response. An apology was offered and there was still no response. However, he did stop and look at me with sad eyes and a hint of a smile. Jake still had not spoken when he looked at the warts on my outstretched hand. I asked again if he could make them go away.

After what seemed an eternity, he took my hand and looked at the warts. He told me to take a lock of my hair and put it under a rock where the rain came off the corner of the roof of the house and splattered on the rock. After I had done what Jake told me to do, I was then instructed to forget about the warts. Tater Jake left without another word and his instructions were followed just as he had directed. I felt rather silly and was skeptical about the whole affair, but did, in fact, forget the incident. I did not give it another thought until one day something drew attention to my hands. Lo and behold the warts were gone!

I ran to show Mother who was properly impressed, but I was overjoyed and convinced that Tater Jake had made the warts disappear. A modern day doctor may have given the same advice, but who knows? It was a lesson learned that would never be forgotten.

The earliest memories are sketchy at best, and they were centered around my mom. Our small log house had two and a half rooms that were always spotless and there was a warm coziness that reflected care in making the house a home. Cleanliness was something that children learned early, and we were conscious about not tracking dirt and mud on the floor. I also learned the necessity of taking care of belongings, which included clothes. Cleanliness was not taken for granted and one never left home to appear in public unless they had been scrubbed and were dressed in clean clothes.

The house was situated on the south side of a ravine that had been carved out through erosion from wind and water. A creek continued to shape the long, deep, narrow valley as it had for thousands of years. There was a distinct difference in the two sides of the ravine, or "hollow" as it was referred to. The house was situated on the south side for good reason. It was especially apparent in winter because the snow and ice lingered much longer on the north side of the hollow.

A tall fir tree stood as a lonely sentinel on the side of the hollow where the winter snow appeared to take forever to leave. It was the only tree of its kind in the whole mountainside. I recalled sitting at the window and gazing out at the regal looking tree which was devoid of branches except for the very top. Each time I looked at the tree, I could not help thinking how utterly lonely the majestic conifer appeared to be. The scene just appeared to be the definition of lonely. I also remembered how sad it was when some men bought the tree and cut it down for lumber. It was one of a kind and I thought it would last forever. I learned that not many things lasted forever.

Mother suffered with a heart disease caused by rheumatic fever from when she was a child. Raising four children and shouldering all the responsibility of making a home for the family in a time when there were no modern conveniences to lighten the workload was a heavy burden. An example of just how difficult the work could be is demonstrated by describing the wash day: Monday was wash day and it began right after Della had cooked breakfast for Lawson and sent him off to work in the mines at four o'clock in the morning. My job was to gather wood for two fires to be used to heat large tubs of water. The tubs were set up near the creek and a large spring so the water would not need to be carried for a long distance. Three tubs were aligned closely together with fires under two of them and cold water in the third one. It might be described as a three cycle wash. The first tub with boiling water was the wash cycle and the second and third ones were the rinse cycles.

The white clothes were washed first. They were placed in the tub with boiling water and a strong lye soap and allowed to soak. A wooden paddle or a handle from a broom was used to stir the clothes until they were judged to be clean. The clothes were lifted from the boiling, soapy water with the paddle or broomstick and placed in the second tub of hot water for the first rinse. If deemed necessary, the clothes were subjected to a scrubbing with the washboard. The clothes were rinsed and wrung out by hand, placed in the third tub, and rinsed a second time.

The second rinsing was necessary to remove the strong lye soap completely. The number of times the process was repeated depended upon the number of loads of clothes that needed to be washed. The boiling water and the rinse water had to be changed several times during the process. One can only imagine how much energy was expended to wring out the clothes by hand and it was done at least twice for each load of clothes. Dad's work clothes had to be washed at least twice. Can you just imagine what mom's hands were like at the end of wash day? It gives new meaning to the phrase, "rubbed her fingernails to the quick." Homemade starch was added to the last rinse which increased the time it took to iron the clothes. The iron was in fact made of iron and was heated on the stove. The iron had a wooden handle to avoid getting burned.

The clean clothes were hung on the clothesline to dry and all that was left to do was the ironing. Some of that chore would probably have to wait until the next day because Dad would soon be home expecting dinner to be on the table. The evening meal was called supper and the noon meal was called dinner. Dinner was usually the large meal of the day, especially if prepared for the men who labored in the fields. Ironically, the men who worked in the mines in darkness carried dinner buckets with hefty meals to build energy for their labor intensive jobs.

Mom's noon meal, if she got one, on wash day was eaten on the run. Her day was not finished until the dishes were washed and stored away and the children put to bed. Her day didn't end when darkness descended, but with no electricity and only a kerosene lamp for light, their lives were planned around the daylight hours. Even so, her day started at three o'clock in the morning and lasted until well after darkness settled. The days of the week that excluded wash day were filled with work in the fields and garden, cleaning the house, canning fruits and vegetables, and caring for the needs of the family. Life in the coal mining region of southwestern Virginia was difficult for most everyone, but especially for the average working men and women.

Livelihood for most people came through a job in the coal mines. They worked and lived from paycheck to paycheck. Payday was always welcome, but when the groceries and other necessities of life that had been charged at the company store during the week were deducted, there was very little left for other staples. In fact, many miners were over drafted and the deficit was carried over to the next pay period. Tennessee Ernie Ford's lament "I Owe My

Soul to the Company Store" was a sad commentary for most miners. Is it any wonder that a two cent raise on a can of lard, which was a cooking staple, was cause for a near revolution?

The family income was usually supplemented by farming the land, if one was fortunate to own some land. The extent of the farming depended upon the available manpower, which was wives, children, and those who did not work in the mines or other jobs associated with the mines. Depending on the size of the workforce, it was possible to raise a garden, plant a field of corn, potatoes, or beans and cultivate fruit trees. A family was truly fortunate to own a cow, some pigs, and a brood of chickens. Milk from the cow, eggs from chickens, meat from livestock, and fruits and berries from the orchard was the difference between a comfortable living and poverty.

The key was to own a piece of land. Fortunately, Mom's persistence netted the family a few acres of land. The house and land on which the family lived was rented from Daniel Clevinger. She urged Dad to purchase part of the land estimated to be twenty plus acres from the Clevingers for eight hundred dollars. It was a lot of money, especially at that time, but it proved to be a good investment. Lawson was reluctant to go into debt to purchase the property and only at her insistence did he relent, and the deal was struck. Faced with one of those instances of a life-changing decision of major proportions, the family chose to take the path less travelled.

They were now a part of the landed aristocracy. Well hardly, but the commitment was made and roots were firmly planted in Meeting House Branch. What a blessing this proved to be! This piece of land was a safe haven for the family because Mom and Dad dared to take a leap of faith. Della was the strength behind that faith. She believed that God would take care of them if they did their part. Her faith manifested itself in many ways even in the difficult times in which we were living.

Della's dream was to see me graduate from high school and go to college. It was a dream that seemed to be improbable, if not impossible, and it was reaching for the stars. She lived long enough to see me reach the first part of that dream. I was going to graduate from the seventh grade and go to high school. She was so proud that she took money that had been given to her for a dress and bought a new shirt for me to wear to the graduation. Little did she know that her dreams would be tested sooner than either one of us could have imagined.

I was twelve years old and the world was my oyster. Every day was exciting and I wanted to explore all of it. I loved to explore the wonders of nature and spent most of the time in the mountains or in the clear sparkling waters of the Levisa River. Later, the river would become polluted when the coal companies released the waste water that was used to clean the coal into the river. It distressed me to see the effects of the pollution and the devastation of the fish population. Mom spent as much time with me as she could and tried to explain what was happening to the environment. She talked to me about many things and I was eager to learn. She shared her dreams for me and hoped they would be my dreams.

Reading was basic and essential for success, so she read to me at every opportunity. Books were at a premium and there was no money to purchase reading material. The only books available were an old set of Compton Encyclopedias. A traveling book salesman convinced her to purchase a set of religious books on credit. She caught a lot of criticism, but she argued that the children needed books to read. She won the argument when she insisted the children needed reading material, especially books about God.

The other source of reading material consisted of comic books or "funny" books as they were called. We enjoyed all kinds of comic books and read them from cover to cover. I especially enjoyed the Prince Valiant ones since they had the most words to read. The primary source of the comic books was from Granny Haley. She worked for people "in town," and when their children were finished with them she brought them home rather than throw them away. The children would wait at the front gate every evening to see whether or not she had brought another treasure. Sometimes I caught fish for her in exchange for the books.

Readers of this document need to be aware that this work is not a piece of historical research. However, there are instances where a number of resources corroborate the facts, and it becomes more than just selective memory.

My sister Peggy remembers another source of comic books. The Norfolk and Western Railroad, now the Norfolk and Southern, ran by the house to transport coal from the mines to ports in Norfolk, Virginia. The tracks were only twenty yards from the house. The children waited anxiously each day for the train to pass so they could wave at the engineer who ran the train and the conductor who rode in the little red caboose at the end of the train. Whatever activity they were engaged in could wait until the passing of the train.

One day the conductor threw a comic book to them and a long lasting relationship was cemented. The man in the little red caboose had gained a daily audience. The children were anxious to see whether or not each new day would bring a comic book, or would they watch disappointedly as the caboose and the conductor rode off into the sunset?

Peggy provided an interesting bit of information that documents this event. She was talking to a friend about this document and happened to mention the fascination of the children for the conductor and the red caboose. The conversation sparked his memory and he told her about a discussion with the conductor who remembered a rag tag group of children who waited each day to see if he would throw them a comic book. The conductor's name was D. M. Hutchinson, and he worked forty years on the railroad. A link to the past authenticated one of the escapades of the Stiltner clan.

Della loved all of her children, but she concentrated on teaching her son as much as possible. It was as though there was an urgency to prepare for an uncertain future. She read to me and shared her dreams for me. She cautioned against allowing plans and dreams to be destroyed by "bad girls," and she also cautioned about ruining the reputation of "good girls." It was as close as she ever came to discussing sex with her only son.

I was devoted to Mother and depended upon her almost exclusively since Dad was away from home. He worked long hours in the mines and on the weekend he went out to be with his friends. Della never complained, at least not where the children could hear, about her lot in life. She accepted her role as mother and wife with no misgivings and had a great philosophy on life; "Accept the things that cannot be changed and make the best of the changes that can be affected. Perhaps, a hardship today may prepare one for greatness tomorrow."

The cold days of January 1948 served as the venue for the birth of Patricia Gail, who completed the family. I had listened to Mother about what was happening and knew that a baby was growing inside her. My only problem with the event was to reconcile the explanation that some people offered which was that they were going "to buy a baby."

It was a happy time, but did not give a hint about the impending event that would require attention to decisions over which we had no control. We were to arrive at a crossroads which would change our lives forever. We were soon to know what it would be like to lose the cornerstone of our very foundation.

SHATTERED DREAMS

R eaching for the stars and dreaming dreams seemed so far from reality that it bordered on the impossible. As impossible as it appeared, the focus was on dreams. They guided me through attempts to reach beyond myself. There were times when everything was right with the world and I was truly happy. However, my world was soon to be shaken to the roots.

Patricia was born in January and the family was eager to help care for her. She was healthy and active, but the added workload for our mother started to take its toll. She spent the remainder of the summer in and out of the Matte Williams Hospital in Richlands, Virginia. She was in the hospital for two or three weeks and would go home when she recuperated. The doctors urged her to rest and take care of herself. That advice fell on deaf ears because she would not stay in bed with so much work to do. It would prove to be the prelude to a life-changing situation with tremendous implications.

The problem was lack of understanding on the part of everyone, including the doctors. Her heart had been badly damaged by rheumatic fever when she was a child. It is fairly certain that with modern knowledge and technology she would have lived a full and healthy life. Not unexpected, she spent time working, which proved to be too much for her weakened heart. My concern for Mother became more troublesome as summer turned to fall. I felt in my heart that she was not getting better, and her time in the hospital was getting to be more frequent. The sequence of events leading up to and including her death is a blur. It is like those last days were not real and I walked around with no real purpose in life. However, I jumped at the chance to go with Dad to see her. The visit to the hospital was so vivid that I never forgot it. She had been in the hospital for two weeks when I was asked if I would like to see her. I was overjoyed at the possibility. Little did I know that this was one of those instances when loved ones were invited to visit one last time.

Joy turned to apprehension when we entered the hospital and saw her in an oxygen tent having difficulty breathing. At her urging, I went to the bedside and took her outstretched hand. She tried to put me at ease as she smiled and said, "You are so brown. You must have been out in the sun." For the next few minutes, I fought back the tears; I had been forewarned not to cry when we saw her.

As I left the room, she assured me that everything would be alright and she would be home soon.

The ride home was subdued and everyone was lost in their own thoughts. Deep down everyone knew that things were not alright, but hoped and prayed that she would soon be well. The visit to see her was near the end of the week, and the following Sunday morning I was sitting on a logging ramp that gave line of sight for at least one-half a mile. From this vantage point I could see the long expanse of the Norfolk and Western railroad that ran by the house. It was a bright, sunny September day and it seemed that I could see forever. What I saw was a lone figure coming toward me at a very slow pace. As the figure came nearer, I realized that it was Aunt Ruby, who was wife to Uncle Johnny. Her pace slowed and became more labored as she approached. I knew in my heart that Mother was dead even before Aunt Ruby confirmed it with the words, "She's gone." My world was never the same.

Everyone was affected by the death of Mom, but no one more acutely than I. I had never faced anything like this and I was devastated. The surreal environment created by the services that were conducted in the small living room of the house where so many happy hours had been spent left me wondering if it was really happening. I finally gathered enough courage to look into the casket to see an ashen-grey pall on her face and realized I had talked with her only days ago: "Why me Lord?" It is a refrain that is expressed many times, but when it is one's anchor in this world there is nothing to do except cry and pray for God's help.

Changes in the lifestyle of the family were inevitable, but it took some time to grasp the magnitude of this unexpected and tragic event in our lives. I became somewhat of a recluse. At first there was the shock of losing Mother, and then I was angry at God. Why did someone so good and kind have to die when there were so many bad people still living? Anger was replaced by an ache that did not soon go away and influenced the decisions that had to be faced.

The death of a loved one, especially a mother, is a life-changing experience of the first magnitude. Celebrate life and let loved ones know that you care for them while they are living. Grandmother Stiltner always asked people to give her flowers while she was still living, not after she was dead. God says, "'Honor thy father and thy mother'– which is the first commandment with a promise – that it may go well with you and that you may enjoy long life on earth" (Ephesians 6:2). How I wished I could have the opportunity to do just that.

PICKING UP THE PIECES

The tragedy of Mom's death at only thirty-three years old had a deep and lasting effect on the whole family. There was no one to kiss the scrapes and bruises away. Now, our lifestyle changed drastically. As difficult as it was for the children, it was even more devastating for Dad. His job in the mines was our livelihood, and now he must also care for four young children. I was twelve years old, Sister Peggy was ten, Ruby was eight, and Patricia was nine months old.

Several attempts were made to find a mature lady to move in with the family and, essentially, become a mother and housekeeper. After seven or eight attempts to find someone to fill this impossible role, we found ourselves at a crossroads. A decision was rendered and a path was chosen as a last resort. The choice had major consequences and implications that made for a rocky road. It impacted the lives of all family members as well as many people around them. The person who was affected the most was Peggy. The decision was like a bombshell when it was announced that she was to drop out of school and become a surrogate mother to the other children. No amount of persuasion or crying was going to change the decision.

Try as he may, Dad still had problems coping with a young family and working to support them. He did keep us together, but he was like a lost soul seeking answers to questions for which mortals could only speculate. He never remarried and we were forced to be participants in a different environment which hastened maturity. As a result of this maturity, we developed an attitude of confidence, which was an asset as we faced the uncertainties of life without a mother. It brought us together and led to a bond that has lasted throughout our lives.

We, as a family, also bonded with two of our many cousins, Lillian Ratliff and Keaster Davis. Lillian lived with her Grandmother Haley and Grandfather Arthur whose house was only a half mile away. Keaster, or Nick as he was called, lived with his family on the other side of the river. Together, they shared love and support that helped to build their character and confidence as they struggled to address the problems that arose from the loss of a loved one. We grew up without much supervision, and as could be expected, probably got into more mischief than we would have under ordinary circumstances.

It has been established earlier that coal miners and their families had to supplement their income by working in the gardens and fields. The workforce for this activity consisted mostly of the women and children who were old enough to help. It was not uncommon to expect children to drop out of school when they became old enough to help with the chores. There was some rule or law which said that children could not drop out of school until they were sixteen years old. The law was not enforced so the dropout rate was high as youngsters reached thirteen or fourteen years of age.

Education was not a high priority for many in rural areas and our family was no exception. To my knowledge, Aunt Alta was the only one from either side of the family to advance past the seventh grade; she went on to graduate from high school. I became the first family member of the Stiltner/Keen clan to advance past the twelfth grade. Matriculation in the eighth grade in September of 1948 proved to be a pivotal time in the quest for an education.

It was a year of historical significance because time in school was increased by one year. Students could no longer matriculate from elementary school directly to high school. Instead, they would spend a year of transition that was called, oddly enough, the eighth grade. Needless to say, the change was met with mixed emotions. Many people looked at graduation from elementary school as the time to drop out of school to start helping the family. To some, it was an innovative way to help students make the transition from elementary school to high school. To others, it was just a scheme to keep students in school for an extra year. This radical change in the curriculum was a hotly debated issue, but it was adopted in time to prevent passage into high school for one more year.

School curriculum was not an issue as far as Lawson was concerned. He had four young children to contend with and mountains to climb. He was determined to keep the family together and to begin to consider the problems that confronted them. Since school was of little value to him, the next potential crisis was announced. He reminded me of my responsibility to help "carry the load." He was tentative, but his meaning was unmistakably clear when he asked, "Don't you think you have had enough schooling?"

I was dumbfounded and managed to say that I did not want to drop out of school. It was the first time that I openly disagreed with Dad, and the first time I thought about running away from home. I was not ready to abandon the dreams that Mother and I had envisioned. Her faith had never been more evident as I stood waiting, fearfully, for Dad to make the decision that would have a profound effect on my future. I tried to strengthen my case by reminding him that Mother wanted me to graduate from high school and go to college. To his credit and my relief, he asked me to think about it.

Perhaps it was selfish of me, but the more I thought about it the more resolute I became. Somehow, some way, I was going to pursue those dreams. The next few days were filled with anxiety, but Dad must have seen the determination in my face and he simply let the issue drop. It was as if Mom was reaching out from the grave to influence the decision that was so painfully being considered. Her faith provided the strength to allow me to rise to heights that both of us desired but neither could envision completely.

In retrospect, I realized that the chance to reach for the stars probably came at the expense of Peggy's dreams. I could have dropped out of school and helped with the work of raising the other sisters and it's possible that Peggy might have been able to return to school. Was it God's hand leading us in this difficult time at a crossroads, or was it stubborn and selfish pride on my part that set the direction of our lives?

I often felt guilty and wondered how our lives would have been changed had my decision been to drop out of school and assume my responsibility. God does not orchestrate the lives of people, but He does help in the struggle to bring some order and stability to people's lives in times of difficulty. Still, I wonder: "What if?"

Grandfather Keen kept some cows and horses, which made it necessary to maintain several hay barns, stalls, corn cribs and some pasture land. It also provided a great area to play. The venue for play was not the safest or the most pleasant smelling they could have chosen. Lillian and I can attest to the folly of disturbing a yellow jackets nest at one of the barns. There was also a very large orchard with many varieties of apples, pears, and fences draped with grape vines that yielded delicious fruit. I can almost taste the mouthwatering delight called the June Apple and the Polly Apple.

At any given day, we could be found in the orchards, the barns, or the creek that were used as the venue for play.

The house was off limits because Aunt Sarah kept it so clean that we could have eaten off the floor. She didn't want it messed up, so we just gave the house a wide berth. On rainy days we were extra careful not to carry mud into the house.

Forgetting the death of Mother was not easy, but we drew strength from each other. We kept busy, which helped, and were sad for a long time. I am reconciled to my mom's death, but there is an empty place in my heart that will always be with me.

AN INTERLUDE

Memories of the early years are bittersweet and I chose to digress a bit to include a wonderful interlude that happened years later. Sisters Ruby, Patricia, and I were enjoying a visit to Peggy's house in Grundy when someone asked about the old home place of the Keen family where they had enjoyed so much time together. We decided to walk the three quarters of a mile back into the mountains to see what it looked like. The old house had been torn down, the grapevines were gone, the apple orchard had long since been destroyed, and the only thing that remained was the old chimney and the old beech tree where we had played as children. It was truly one of the most absolutely wonderful times that provided a great memory for all of us.

The time spent together prompted me to write a short account of the day and call it "The Old Beech Tree." I shared it with my sisters and Pat returned to the spot later to take a picture from which she painted a scene of the "Old Beech Tree" and the chimney. The painting, which was presented to me for my birthday, hangs in my little corner of the world. I decided to share the moment and included it as a vignette. No attempt was made to clean up the grammar since the text was done at the spur of the moment and the extemporaneous expression of love just spilled out. Here are the memories that were shared as we enjoyed one of the most memorable visits back to the old home place.

THE OLD BEECH TREE

The day began as it had for many years for the old
Beech Tree. It was the kind of day that makes one
want to be alive, unless like for the old beech tree
that stood vigil over a once thriving homestead,
it was just another interlude in a monotonous
procession toward eventual oblivion.

The old tree couldn't be criticized too harshly
for a lack of enthusiasm. After all, he had watched
over several generations of the Keen family

who had occupied the old grey but pleasant looking house which had stood nearby. He had provided shade for happy children at play as well as family friends who came to visit.

The path that wound its way from the mouth of the creek and up the hollow to the old house had been wide and well worn. On occasion even trucks and cars had been driven up to what came to be known as the Arthur Keen place. Alas, the bustling activity came to an end shortly after old man Arthur died.

The old house was torn down and only the mud and stone chimney remained. The path, no longer traveled, had been obscured by weeds and bushes. Now each day stretched into the next with the only sounds being the rustling of the leaves in the breeze. The old tree was left with only memories. It was not so easy to share the happy times as well as the sad times of so many people and then be left completely alone.

We remembered old man Arthur, his children, grandchildren, and great grandchildren who called him Poppy with his unlimited patience and love for his family. Then there was Haley, his wife whose cooking made Sunday dinner an occasion to remember. It was not unusual for thirty or more people to congregate from miles around to enjoy some of "Aunt Haley's" chicken and dumplings. Haley and Arthur were blessed with a large family, and when Jenny, Stella, Ellen, Cordelia, Sarah, Alta, Johnny, and Milton were home with their families there was quite a crowd even without friends and neighbors. Hardly a day passed when there wasn't a number of children running and playing around the trunk of the old tree. As the years passed, however, members of the family moved away or passed into obscurity leaving only memories of an era past. *The only consolation*, thought the old tree, *is that no one is around to carve their initials in my bark.* But then thinking wistfully, he mused, *maybe it would be worth it just to have someone pay attention to me*

and appreciate the cool shade under my
spreading branches again. Oh well, he sighed,
there is a gentle breeze and it's a good day
for basking in the sun.

Suddenly, the tranquil
world of the old tree was interrupted. *What is*
all that noise? Apprehensively, and with a bit
of anticipation, he watched as a small truck
made its way, with some difficulty, through
the weeds and brush that had taken the road.
Finally, the truck could go no further and five
people got out and proceeded slowly up the path.
They are probably going on up the holler to
look at some of the old mines, the old tree
speculated. *But no they are making their way*
across the creek and coming right at me.
Besides miners don't dress like these people
are dressed.

The suspense was overwhelming
as the old tree strained to identify his new
visitors. *That guy swinging the weed cutter*

looks familiar. Of course! He is that fellow
Mike who has some dogs that he keeps
somewhere down the creek. He is the son-in
law of one of the Stiltner girls who used to
play here as a youngster. What? Did that blond
fellow call one of the girls Peg? Yes! It is It is!
That is one of Cordelia's and Lawson's children.
All the kids called her Peg, but her name was
really Dorothy. Oh, it is good to see her!
She's older, but the sparkle is still in her eyes,
and I'll bet she could be talked into a game
of hide and seek without too much trouble.
I know she is the only one of the children who
stayed close to the home place, but I haven't
seen her in such a long time that it was difficult
to recognize her.

As the old tree searched his
memory for a clue as to who the other three
people were, he overheard Peg call out to Ruby
to watch the mud near the creek. Could it be
that all of Cordelia and Lawson's children had
come back for a visit? It must be. There had

been one boy and three girls – Peg, Ruby and
Patricia. The boy and Peg were blond and fair
like their mother and the other two girls had
dark complexion like their dad.

The four came
abreast of the old tree and he realized that
although they were a little grey in spots, they
were indeed the same eager beavers who had
run barefoot past this very spot many years
ago. Harold, the one they called Buddy, was the
oldest and perpetrated most of the mischief
they got caught up in. Ruby was younger than
Peg, but would not be left out of the activities
that included catching crawdads, playing in
the hayloft, and hunting hickory nuts in the
ocean of leaves that fell and accumulated in
the fall of each year.

Cordelia had died at a young
age and left a young baby named Patricia
to be cared for by Lawson and the three
other children. They grew up together and

despite the steady diet of mashed bananas
for Pat they survived and developed a
closeness that is seldom found in brothers
and sisters. How good it is to see them all
together again. The old tree basked in the
memory of the four of them and felt a part
of the bond of love that bound them together.

He didn't feel at all like an intruder as they
stood looking at the remains of the old house,
each transfixed for a while and lost in their
memories. Their faces reflected what must
have been a mixture of joy and sadness as they
remembered the good times as well as the pain
of growing up and the loss of those who were
so dear to them. They reminisced about the
past for a while, joked about the bugs and
snakes that might be lurking about, and
finally said farewell to a part of their lives
that can only be visited through memories.

The old tree almost burst with happiness as
they slowly made their way past him on their

way down to the creek. Each of them paused
to caress his trunk and to peer once more into the
dark hole in his side that had intrigued them in
the days of their youth. For a day that had
started out so uneventfully, it had turned into
a glorious day. He had revived memories as
he knew they had, to keep from being lonely
for a long time.

This interlude may have significance only for me and
my sisters, but it should remind everyone that time and
tide wait for no man. A lifetime is a fleeting moment in the
macrocosm and scheme of things of which we are a part.
Man is in this world, and in the blink of an eye he is gone.
Do not wait until tomorrow to touch someone you love.

BUILDING CONFIDENCE AND CHARACTER

W e were not without some supervision, but with Dad working, we were left to play, experiment, roam, and experience life as we chose. It would prompt some neighbors to say that no good would come of those children running wild. It didn't matter that we did not have a room full of toys to play with since a stickweed or an old mop served as a trusty steed to chase outlaws. The addition of a Roy Rogers or Gene Autry cap pistol for me and a doll for the girls at Christmas added to already rich and active imaginations. We were poor and didn't know it. Still, we managed to mature into pretty responsible adults who were guided by a mother's early teachings.

We swam in the river when Dad was at work and did not even think of the danger. He warned us not to go near the river and we knew his wrath would descend upon us if we disobeyed, so we made certain that we got out of the water in time for our hair to dry and to get dirty before he got home.

A near tragedy sobered us and caused us to be more careful when in the water. Sister Ruby had not yet learned to swim and wandered out from the riverbank where she was in over her head. I noticed she was struggling and drowning. I had presence of mind enough to know that had I jumped in to rescue her, we both would have drowned. I dived into the water, swam around behind her, and pushed her to the shore. Why did I have benefit of such logical knowledge when it was needed? Only the angels know.

This incident reminded me of another very important source of strength for the family. It had to do with what can be called "divine intervention." I was later convinced that angels were constant companions who guided and protected us. How else could I explain occurrences that turned potential disasters into good fortune? Some of these instances are not unique, but give insight into the belief that there is a higher power watching over us. That power is God; who assures that all things are possible though Christ, who strengthens us.

Somehow we conquered the mountains and life became bearable. There were more obstacles to be overcome and each day offered strength to prevail. Some of our efforts were supported by the help of good Samaritans and time did heal the wounds that were inflicted through the loss of our mother.

Adversity was a constant with us and we faced the problems that life served up and seemed to grow stronger with each test that was encountered. Each challenge was met with determination; we vowed to stay focused on our goals. I considered myself fortunate to have such wonderful and caring sisters and cousins.

First cousin Keaster went to train as a heavy equipment operator and was very successful. First cousin Lillian graduated from Pikeville College in Kentucky and worked as a guidance counselor and teacher, Ruby graduated from King College and Virginia Tech to become a very successful teacher, coach, and high school administrator. Patricia graduated from Concord College and became a successful librarian and teacher. I was fortunate enough to culminate my formal education with a Ph.D. from Georgia State University. Sister Peggy never attended college, but she educated herself and is more knowledgeable and smarter than all the rest of us put together. She has every right to feel slighted, but there is not a jealous bone in her body, and she will eagerly tell you that there are not enough worldly goods that will buy the love and joy she has in her God and family. She is a saint.

THREE FOR ONE

There were three incidents that occurred early in life which potentially could have altered or even ended my life. I remember the events as if they happened yesterday. However, the concept of what I choose to call "selective memory" is always a possibility. One selects and sometimes embellishes or diminishes the facts surrounding particular events in life. They may even omit unpleasant aspects of the story, such as why there were wet pants following a particular incident. The incident may have happened as it is remembered or may have been heard so many times that I think I experienced it. At any rate, the incidents did occur, causing the facts to be prefaced with the statement, "cross my heart and hope to die if it is not the truth."

These three incidents have been grouped together because they have a tendency to experience embellishment each time they are recalled. The time frame included the years when I was five, six, and seven years old. The events actually happened, but the snake may have been four feet rather than five feet long and the train may have been going thirty miles an hour rather than fifty, and well...you know. We remember it well.

The first "recollection" shows the fearless nature of a curious youngster. The time was early spring because the grass was green and the flowers were in bloom. The time of year was evident because the large pile of coal used for heating the house had been consumed and only "slack," or fine particles of coal, were left. Like any child, I was drawn to the area where I could get the dirtiest in the least amount of time.

Another one of God's creatures was also attracted to the inviting warmth generated by the sun shining on the black coal. A copperhead snake was coiled up in the middle of the depleted coal pile. The place was large enough for both of us so we shared the space. I am told that I must have been curious to find out how the new "friend" wanted to play. I began to scoop up the coal residue and let it spill on the head of the snake.

The interaction with the new playmate was short-lived when Mother, who had been sweeping the porch, saw what was happening. Her reaction was one of sheer terror. She covered the space between us in record time and jerked me quickly away from the snake. She hailed a neighbor, Clyde Looney, who happened to be on his way to work in his garden. He came with his hoe and killed the snake. The particulars of the incident were shared with family and friends. Each time it was repeated it took on more significance.

Some people were convinced that the snake had hypnotized me, and others knew that I had been charmed. For a young child who had known no fear before, it was the beginning of a new emotion that would grow into an appreciation of the wonders of nature. It was the beginning of something that would be a constant companion. I learned what fear was all about that day as I was admonished and convinced that the snake was bad and could hurt me. I understood later what God meant when he said to the serpent that man, "will crush your head you will strike his heel" (Genesis 3:14). The incident was not a life-changing situation, but it was a learning experience.

I was the first grandchild of Grandpa and Grandma Stiltner and Grandma and Grandpa Keen. To say that I was favored would be somewhat of an understatement. Of course, I reveled in the good fortune to which I had been born. It was great to be spoiled by eleven aunts and uncles. On Dad's side there were five uncles; George, Charlie, David, Kermit, and Burns. On Mother's side there were two uncles: Johnny and Milton; and five aunts: Jenny, Stella, Ellen, Sarah, and Alta. After that, it became complicated with at least eleven aunts and uncles by marriage. When the families came together for some occasion it proved to be a happening.

I do not remember whether it was my desire to stay with Dad's parents or if it was done out of necessity to give

Mom a little help with Peggy and Ruby. That decision was made for me and resulted in much of my early life being spent with grandparents and uncles. I was definitely in a male dominated environment for the impressionable years of my life. At any rate, when it came time to enter the first grade, everyone agreed that it would be best for me to stay with the grandparents and uncles and attend Cedar Grove Elementary School. It certainly would be better than going to that big city school in Grundy. Besides, Uncle Burns, who was in the fifth grade, was there to protect me. It was another decision that was made for me. I often speculate on how it influenced my early life and how it may have been different had I been sent to live with other grandparents in a female dominated environment. I will never know.

The decision had been rendered and the school bell rang to mark the first day of school. The two room schoolhouse opened up a whole new vista for me. I will never forget the smell that greeted us when we stepped inside the room that housed the first through fourth grades. The smell was from the heavy, dark oil that was used to treat the floors. Its purpose was to protect the floor and to keep the dust down. In the winter, the students were kept warm by a large potbellied stove that got so hot it glowed. If your seat was close to the stove it was too warm and if you sat in the back of the room it was freezing.

With the coming of spring, the stoves were not needed, but heat was still a problem. There was no air conditioning, and the odor of the treatment of the floors was combined with the odors of body heat and perspiration to provide a new sensation to the environment.

Recess in midmorning and mid afternoon was chaotic to say the least. Students had fifteen minutes to spend on the playground and everyone played a modified game of baseball. That is, if you could get through the line to get a drink of water from an outside pump. There was a well-established procedure by which students got a drink of water. The first student in line, who was usually one of the older children, had the second in line to man the pump while he cupped his hands and got a drink. He would in turn pump water for the second in line. After each got a drink they would man the pump for the next in line until everyone got a drink. The first in line got to play ball, but if you were very far back in line you were lucky to get a drink before it was time for the bell to ring.

So it went for the first and second grades. The early years were spent with Grandma and Grandpa Stiltner, and I started the third grade at Cedar Grove School in the fall. The five uncles were living at home and delighted in telling stories that they swore were true. They were good storytellers and I was convinced that around every rock or building there was some kind of a ghost ready to jump me, especially at night. Their attempts to scare me were so successful that I was terrified to go out in the dark. That might explain why I am reluctant to sleep in a room that is devoid of some light. The constant hazing by the uncles Charlie, George, and David was done with no malice, but it gave new meaning to the concept of homesick for an eight year old. Uncles Kermit and Burns did not enter into the activities, but they did nothing to discourage the friendly spooking.

I loved my uncles, but the uncomfortable feeling growing inside of me due to the entire situation, coupled with the desire to be with Mom and Dad, led me to make a difficult decision. I announced to the uncles and to my grandparents that I was going home. They pleaded but I had made up my mind; I was going home. The next hurdle was to determine how to make the trip home to Meeting House Branch. It should be noted that the distance was only five or six miles between Grandpa Stiltner's house and Mom and Dad's house but to an eight-year-old youngster it might as well have been a hundred miles.

The thought of returning home brought up dear memories of Grundy, a metropolis with a population of approximately three thousand people. It was located two to three miles further north from my home on route 360, which was an additional five to six miles from where I was at the time. Grundy had that small-town feel to it, wedged between the Levisa River and the mountains. It gave new meaning to the phrase "you can't miss it." Although it was difficult to miss the town in a directional sense, I sure missed it a lot. Grundy was a small town and I loved it.

The announcement that I was going home to see my mom and dad met with little support, but I was adamant. I was informed that there was no one to take me home. I announced that I would go by myself, but kept hoping that someone would agree to take me home. The stalemate was broken when someone produced a dime to ride the bus to Meeting House Branch. The bus was a part of the Black and White Transit Company that ran from the town of Grundy to Harman Junction a round-trip of twenty miles. Uncle

Charlie took me over the railroad tracks and across the river on what must have been the most precarious swinging bridge anyone ever walked on. He hailed the bus and it came to a halt with the air brakes screeching. I climbed up into the bus, gave the driver a dime and found an empty seat. I was on the way home.

Uncle Charlie had told me that I should pull the chord above my seat when the bus got to Meeting House Branch. The only problem was that the bus was on the highway and the house was across the river. The only way to get from one side of the river to the side on which Mom's house was located was by boat. The house was a half mile from the river, so I knew that I could not call for mom or dad to bring the boat to carry me across. I decided to try my luck with the closest neighbor who lived a mile from the house, but was within earshot of the river. I pulled the cord and the big black and white bus came to an abrupt stop. I was almost home.

I climbed down the embankment to the edge of the river and began to yell, "Bring me the boat!" The Delmon Looney family had a house full of boys and girls, any one of whom could have heard the call. They either did not hear or ignored the call for help. I called until my voice was hardly above a whisper. I started to have a feeling of uneasiness begin to creep into my thinking as it became clear that no one was coming to carry me across the river.

The gathering darkness just added to my plight, as I recalled some of the shadowy places that had been brought to life by the ghost stories of my uncles. What had started out as an anticipated joyous homecoming had been replaced by an urgency to achieve the immediate goal – getting across the river. I probably cried a little, but not too much because boys my age were not supposed to cry.

Darkness was fast approaching and the need to reach my objective became more urgent. Did I fail to mention that it was cold? Winter had not yet arrived, but an early cold snap that was not unusual for the mountains had caused some ice to form on parts of the river. The Levisa River was approximately thirty-five to forty yards wide and its depth varied depending on whether you were looking at the deep bodies of water or the shoals. He decided the shoals would be the best bet to reach the other side since there were protruding rocks that could be used as stepping stones. The only problem was the distance from one rock to another was a bit long and one had to take a good jump to make it safely. I hesitated as I considered the next move. It did not take long because the impending darkness left no other options and the attempt to traverse the river began. The trek went well until I reached midpoint of the shoal. The distance to the next rock required a longer jump which was not successful and I ended up in the icy cold water which was up to my neck. There was no danger of drowning since I could swim, but it occurred to me that I might very well freeze to death. All the worldly goods I had brought with me were lost as I slowly made my way across the remaining distance to the other side of the river.

Soaked and freezing, I deposited myself at Mom's front door. To say that she was taken aback would be an understatement. She alternated between anger and relief, but hastened to get me out of the frozen clothes and embraced me in a way that only she could. She said something like, "I will never let you go back except for a visit and I will be with you." It was good to be home.

The episode was significant and may well have been divine intervention to prepare for what was to change my life within the next few years. God works in mysterious ways, His wonders to perform. It was one more test to help develop confidence that would be shaken in the future, but would never desert me.

The following incident was perhaps the most life-altering event that happened. I was five or six years old and remember the incident like it was yesterday, or have I heard the story so many times that I think I remember it? Nevertheless, it did happen and if nothing more it serves as another good topic for oral history.

The family lived within twenty yards of the tracks of the Norfolk and Western Railroad and had been warned repeatedly to stay far away from the tracks. On this particular day I was with Aunt Sarah and it was ok for me to walk on the tracks. I was walking on the very same tracks on which the big black engine rolled. We stopped to rest near an outcropping of rock that had been blasted away to make way for the railroad. One could move carefully to the edge of the precipice and peer over to see the rocks far below. Memory says it was a huge drop to the river, but in reality it was approximately a thirty-five-foot drop and in a child's eyes that was an imposing distance. Still, a fall to the jagged rocks below could cause a serious injury or even death.

It was a beautiful day to enjoy the wonderful gifts of God's world. Aunt Sarah was content to sit on the edge of the cliff and soak up some sun while I played on the railroad tracks. I had wandered up the tracks for a short distance when I heard the unmistakable sound of the big black engine that was pulling a long string of coal cars. I was petrified for a moment and just knew that I was going to be gobbled up by the big black engine.

The train was still some distance away, but I ran as if it was nipping at my heels. I raced back to Aunt Sarah, and, as some versions of the story goes, was so terrified that I would have run over the edge of the cliff to the rocks below had she not grabbed the back strap of my overalls to prevent the fall. You can imagine how the incident grew each time it was recalled and the suspense it created especially the last second grab to save the day. I remember it well.

Of course, there were other events and incidents that helped to mold the personality that was the son of Lawson and Cordelia, brother to Dorothy Lucille, Ruby Virginia, and Patricia Gail, husband to Phyllis Sue, father to Brian Leigh and Christopher Allen, father-in-law to Mary Helon [Molly] and Jeana Adriane, and grandfather to Nathan James, Sara Elizabeth, Jackson Allen and Reese Adriane. Friends and colleagues figured prominently in this evolutionary development, but these are the solid rocks on which I stand. They are a part of all I am or ever will be.

A number of other events influenced and, in some instances, served to alter my personality. The events may have come about as a result of the persistent pursuit of goals or dreams, or may have been occurrences that were unexplained and unexpected that some would consider fate. Personally, I believe things happen for a reason and the God of the universe who knows the very hairs on our head speaks to us through these experiences. He speaks to us in a "still small voice," and if we are attentive, we will know that He is working in our lives. He admonishes and comforts us, "Be still, and know that I am God" (Psalm 46:10).

Big Brother Jim Taking Care of Peggy

THE REST OF THE STORY

Peggy, Ruby, Patricia, and I had innumerable instances where we were obligated to make decisions that led us in many different directions. Each has their own story which should be told. Unfortunately, the primary focus of these vignettes is on my experiences. Insofar as the decisions affect the family, they will be included. This is one of those times.

Peggy became a wonderful "mom" to Pat and she matured into a confident, loving and caring person. She met and married Leonard Matney and they settled on part of the land that Mother and Dad had acquired. They were blessed with three children, Roger, Debbie, and Robin. She and Leonard became members of the Grundy Church of Christ and they literally carried the outreach program on their backs. Unfortunately, the team that everyone looked to for leadership is now provided only by Peggy; Leonard, whose infectious smile will always be remembered, was called to heaven to share that smile.

Peggy and Leonard were delighted when Roger married Susan and had their first grandchild, Matthew. Debbie married Mike Yates and they gave birth to Kristina who in turn married Kenneth Carter and made Peggy and Leonard great grandparents by giving birth to Kory and Kelli. Robin and her husband Richard Cauvel added Adam to the growing family. At Christmas the word is togetherness, as their cozy home serves as the gathering point for the family. Ruby became heir to the role vacated by Peggy as the caretaker of the family, but did not have to drop out of school in order to fulfill her responsibilities. She graduated from high school, earned a college degree from King College, and Master degree from Virginia Tech, became a master teacher of Chemistry and Physics, was a successful basketball coach, and a successful administrator all while raising her own family.

She and husband Harold Kirby had two wonderful children named Jeff and Cindy. Jeff and his wife Trisha made Ruby a proud grandmother to Maddie, Jay, and Henry. Ruby was also grandmother to Cindy's three children, Lee, Lindsey, and Alex. In addition to all her accomplishments, she helped Cindy become a Physical Therapist and care for and guide the three children to earn their college degrees.

Everyone had their misfortunes, but Pat suffered most. She was tossed from pillar to post for most of her life but proved to be as resilient as the rest of the family. She graduated from high school, earned an undergraduate degree from Concord College and a master's degree from Marshall University and was a successful teacher. She and first husband Carl had two sons, Carl Franklin and Brandon. She ended up raising the boys, and after they matured she searched diligently for some meaning for her life. She failed to find the peace and sense of belonging for which she had searched all of her life and died at an early age. Carl Franklin and his wife Harlina added two grandchildren, Joseph Carl and Aaron to the family and Brandon and his wife Regina added Nicholas and Tavia Kelly to the clan. Brandon died in an accident before she was born. All the family had star-crossed and bittersweet lives and each story deserves to be told. Perhaps someone else will take pen and fill in some of the other experiences that have made the family unique.

What happened to cousins Lillian and Nick? Lillian went to Pikeville College in Pikeville, Kentucky, graduated and became a teacher and counselor. She married Dillard Keen who was also a Teacher and very successful basketball coach. Dillard, or "Zeke" as he was called, gained entrance to the family through me. He played basketball at King College and was my roommate. Nick married Evelyn Owens and worked on heavy equipment. Unfortunately, he died at an early age from an unusual malady: he developed a case of hiccups and could not stop and died of a heart attack as a result of the problem.

We four siblings grew up with a minimum of supervision and became successful because of our ability to meet and overcome the obstacles to which we were subjected. We literally pulled ourselves up by the proverbial boot straps. We were not supposed to succeed, but with a lot of help from caring people we prevailed.

A STORY OF PRESEVERANCE

Dreams are up front and personal. They are elusive; may flit in and out of thoughts, but may also provide a solid framework for a great accomplishment. Dreams can be simple or they can be lofty. Little girls dream of being a princess and little boys dream of being a king or a sports hero, but as we grow older our dreams provide benchmarks for more realistic goals and objectives. Dreams are attainable, but may be something for which we strive and cannot reach. Do we dare to dream the "impossible dream;" "to reach for that unreachable star?" Absolutely, we must! The simplest of dreams demand hard work and dedication and a willingness to make adjustments when life dictates.

For some reason when thinking of dreams, visions of fluffy white clouds come to mind. Perhaps it is because I spent many hours on the same rock formations I had tried to leap from in earlier years to escape an encounter with the big black train. A part of that formation was a large granite rock at the river's edge that was user friendly. It was located at a large body of water that had been a gathering pool for logs that had been cut upriver and floated downriver to be processed by a lumbering company. The logs were drawn out of the river and sawed into lumber to be used for building purposes. The sawmill had long since ceased to operate, but it had left an excellent place to fish and swim.

I remember lying on my back on the large boulder, peering up at the white fluffy clouds overhead and letting my mind conjure up dreams of what the future might hold. The dreams included everything from being accepted by my peers, becoming a basketball star, and becoming a successful businessman to travel the world over.

The rock was a refuge, and for a while a very private place. Peggy and Leonard found it and it became a special place for them. If memory serves well, it was on this very same rock that Leonard proposed to her and their life together was as solid as that piece of granite. I was happy to share my little corner of the world where anyone could dream to their heart's desire.

It was impossible to count the number of times that I laid on the rock and gazed up into the blue sky with white fluffy clouds and pictured myself as a member of the Minneapolis Lakers Basketball Team. Visions of winning a ball game never featured a runaway, but it was always a last second shot to win the game. It was during one of those close games that it occurred to me that I should construct a basketball goal and act out my fantasies. The first attempt was a crudely fashioned rim from a tin bucket. It even had a net made of strips of cloth and was attached to the side of the house. The "basketball" was a rubber sponge ball that was three inches in diameter. The backboard was the side of the house and there was very little room to drive in for a layup basket. Nevertheless, I now had an arena that demanded performance rather than a daydream game.

It was a long season and the game had to go on rain or shine. During the season a larger ball was introduced which changed the complexion of the game. It was a rubber air ball that was five inches in diameter and was definitely livelier and sometimes required several last second attempts to win the game. Life in the fast lane was exciting and proceeded on schedule until one day Dad had occasion to look at the side of the house that supported the basketball goal. His reaction may have been different had it not been for the white asbestos siding to which the goal was affixed. Play on the muddy days had left a definite impression. Needless to say, some changes in the venue were required.

Play was suspended for the construction of a new arena. The plans were formulated, but how to convert them into a finished product was the next objective. Working with limited supply of tools, a water birch tree was cut to specifications and rough slats were nailed on it to make a backboard.

All that was needed now was a bucket and a hole in the ground to support the goal. The hole was not a problem, but the rim was another story. An extensive search yielded a small oil drum that had a diameter that was similar to a basketball rim. Memory does not serve well here, but somehow I managed to cut the upper one fourth of the oil drum and nail it to the backboard. The finished product was planted in the ground and declared ready for play. It was beautiful only to the builder.

Play was resumed and several contests were nip and tuck and some impossible shots were made to win games. There were games that featured formidable foes that required several attempts to win, and they were always close and almost never ended in a loss. The season ended when the air literally left the ball. A deflated ball does not help the imagination to any great extent. The season was coming to a close anyway since winter was closing in. Hours on end and in all kinds of weather the game of basketball became almost an obsession. I took every opportunity to have a ball in my hands even if it was less than regulation. Dreams of playing basketball and graduating from high school appeared to be a pipedream. Did I even dare to think that I might be able to reach for the stars?

The spring semester of the eighth grade was pivotal for my basketball aspirations. I was now introduced to the reality of the sport. The ball was regulation and the basket was adjusted to the proper height. However, the venue was much different from the makeshift situation I had at home. I also realized that there was real live competition for opportunities to play. Discouraged at times, but undaunted I seized every opportunity to be involved in basketball. The home venue was now completely inadequate. The ball was not even close to being a basketball. However, fate gave a boost to the aspirations of a struggling would-be basketball player.

Late winter and early spring in southwestern Virginia was the time when the spring rains came to refresh the earth. Occasionally, the rain was enough to cause flooding along the banks of the Levisa River. This particular spring the rain was very abundant. There was so much water that the river became a raging torrent. The river was over flood stage to the point that it was very near the railroad tracks and perilously close to the house. The danger was imminent. It should have been a clear signal to stay far away from the raging waters that were sweeping everything in its path hundreds of miles away. We had been warned against going near the river, but the fascination was too great. I was sitting within ten feet of the river's edge watching all the interesting items coming from upstream. Suddenly, my focus was transfixed on an object that swept all fear aside and caused my heart rate to skyrocket. The object was a full size basketball! I immediately began to run parallel to the swiftly moving river and its precious cargo. As I ran I grabbed anything in sight to throw beyond the floating ball to cause it to move closer to land.

Finally, the current and the rocks moved the ball closer to the river's edge. An excited youngster threw caution to the wind when it caught in some brush near enough to wade out and retrieve the prize. Could it be real? Was it by accident that I had been here at the precise moment to see the ball floating down the river or was it fate? Was I dreaming? Was it a bit of each? At any rate, my joy was overwhelming to actually realize that I had been blessed beyond description. Could life be any sweeter? Should I try to locate the owner? It could have come downriver for forty or fifty miles. I didn't know where to start to find the owner so I decided to keep the prize.

Adjustments were made for the basketball venue to accommodate the new equipment. To say the activity near the basketball goal was increased would be an understatement. There was one significant change in the purpose of the game. The emphasis shifted from a make-believe mode to a more serious focus on practice. The summer was given over to hours of drill that included putting the ball through the hoop and dribbling the ball.

The new objective was to make the ninth grade basketball team. It was an unorganized program. If one desired to play on the team, practice would be scheduled when the gym was not being used, which was almost never, and all were invited to participate. Coaching was done by a volunteer teacher with no instruction or attention to fundamentals. They had two, maybe three, games and very few practice sessions. Playing time was scarce so I concentrated on what I would do if I touched the ball either in the game or in practice. What couldn't be accomplished at school was practiced at home with the new regulation basketball.

I was discouraged, but the desire and dreams of playing basketball never wavered. I continued to try to make my presence felt at every opportunity, which was not easy for a 110 pound five-foot-nine-inch "skinny-miny" superstar (in my perception). I strived to supplement progress at school with practice at home until the regular size basketball gave up the ghost. It finally became deflated and even the strongest imagination could not bring it back to life.

The tenth grade offered a new challenge and opportunity. Aspirations now settled on the lofty goal of playing for the Grundy Golden Wave Junior Varsity Basketball team; sounds impressive doesn't it? The program was definitely more structured, but was still under the direction of a teacher who volunteered to coach the team. The only time available for practice was early in the morning and I vividly remember the cold frosty mornings that I walked a mile to get to the highway to hitchhike a ride to the school to practice. I realized there was another requirement necessary for playing this game. It was called "endurance" and that was my middle name. Through sheer determination and a never-say-die attitude I managed to make the team. It proved to be a bittersweet experience and another mountain to climb.

I survived the cuts, but learned that making the team did not guarantee playing time. It also did not earn a uniform since all uniforms were hand-me-downs from the varsity team. The coach distributed the uniforms to those he considered to be the first team. Unfortunately, he had a limited number of uniforms and he informed the remaining team members that we could share game jerseys if we had basketball shorts. It was not at all what I had dreamed about while lying on that favorite piece of granite.

Feelings of doubt began to creep into my mind and chip away at an already shaky confidence. The negative thoughts were subdued and the search began for some basketball shorts. I did not even remember where they came from, but a pair of bright green and yellow shorts was found. Not what your fashion expert would recommend, but they would have to do. The first game was at home and when the team came out of the locker room to warm up, there I was in all my splendor in the bright green and yellow satin shorts. I couldn't imagine what the fans were saying, but I could feel it. Doubt raised its ugly head again and it was becoming difficult to shake it off.

A voice deep inside kept saying, *give it up, give it up, but if you give up the dream is gone.* Maybe the cold frosty mornings for practice were freezing my brain. The quest was not an obsession because I was working hard to achieve the goal of graduating from high school. The early morning practices continued and I was there when the gym doors opened. I never had to walk the three miles to school because several people who went to work early would stop and give me a lift to town.

There was one particular lady who was very nice and she never passed by without stopping. She worked in town and dropped her twin girls off at school each morning. The twins were in their own element and paid very little attention to me as they rode to town. I didn't have a clue as to what they thought about me; I was just glad to have a ride to get to basketball practice. Perhaps I should have paid more attention because twelve years later I would take one of them as my wife. The very nice lady who was kind enough to help me get to practice on more than one occasion was Mrs. Georgia Shortridge, mother of Phyllis and Betty and destined to be my mother-in-law.

Meanwhile, I was still chasing a dream that was trying to elude me. The away games also had limitations. Transportation was furnished by the coach and older team members who drove their personal cars. The day of the first away game finally arrived, and we were filled with great anticipation. I asked the coach about the time of departure and who would ride with whom. He informed me that the team would gather behind the gym immediately after the school day ended and would be assigned to ride in one of the three cars providing transportation.

I was filled with anticipation and could hardly wait for the last class period to end. It finally ended and I eagerly rushed to the back of the gym only to discover that there was no one around. I thought that I must be the first to arrive so I sat on the steps and waited for the other team members to arrive. Ten minutes passed and I started to have an empty feeling in the bottom of my stomach. I gathered my gear and ran to the front of the school only to see the last car pull out of the school parking lot. I began to run after the car until it became apparent that I had never been included in the travel squad. The coach just couldn't tell me face-to-face that I was not on the traveling team or maybe my green and yellow satin short shorts were too much of an embarrassment.

The time to face reality was overdue and the dream started to slip away as the tears were brimming over my eyelids and down my cheeks. In retrospect, I could relate to singer Peggy Lee when she asks in her song, "Is that all there is?" Yet, I resisted the urge to throw in the towel and admit that the impossible dream, the unreachable star, was truly out of my reach. What was so important about going to school and playing a silly game anyway? Dad said it was time to grow up and assume responsibility at home. Heaven knows I had had enough kicks in the rear to bring me back to earth.

I had arrived at one of those crossroads in life that demanded a response. There was no one to turn to for help and the path I chose would alter life forever. It wasn't just the dream of playing basketball; it was the absurd idea that the son of a poor out-of-work coal miner would ever be able to play basketball, graduate from high school, and go to college. Dad was out of work because the United Mine Workers Association had demanded too much of management, and as a result the mines in southwest Virginia and much of the surrounding area were closed.

Under the leadership of John L. Lewis the union had helped the workers by keeping the wages high with good benefits. The only fly in the ointment was that management, which was largely by absentee ownership from the Northeast, was not going to operate when it was no longer profitable. They had made their millions and the profit margin was not as lucrative as it had been, so they simply closed the operation down. Small independent operators sprang up to fill the need for coal. They were free to mine the coal without the restrictions placed on the "Union Mines." These operations were labeled "scabs" by the men who were loyal to the union. Dad was one of those diehard Union workers and he worked for years doing odd jobs to scratch out a living. It was another mountain to climb by a family that was already weary of fighting uphill battles.

By no means were the people in the area the only ones affected, but that was little consolation. Without the money from wealthy owners who had purchased the mineral rights for ninety-nine years for a song, it was impossible to bring the coal industry back to its former glory. In fact, the economy was so bad that the entire coal mining region was identified as part of "Appalachia," a term that was associated with poverty.

Everyone who lived in Appalachia was not poor, but many people struggled to make ends meet. The conditions could be likened to a fine tapestry. The land was beautiful, the people were happy, coal was king, and times were good. The Appalachian Mountains, once like the majestic peaks of the Rockies, had worn down over many, many years to a less jagged, more friendly and intimate mountain range covered with lush green vegetation. The mountains represented a giant tapestry that encompassed all that was a part of God's world. However, the tapestry developed flaws resulting from greed, misuse, and abuse that marred its beauty and earned it the distinction of being identified with "Appalachia."

The flaws mended in time and the beauty is still there, but for some the poverty remains. It was against this backdrop that the decision about pursuing dreams was made. The odds were not in my favor and the dreams were torn and tattered like the tapestry. No one understood all the ramifications or implications of the environment just described, but I just knew that I was faced with the most critical decision of my life. What was at stake? Chasing the dream of playing basketball was symbolic of my struggles. Giving up was not in my vocabulary; at least it had not been until now. Not only would I be giving up on my dreams and aspirations, but also on the dreams and expectations of my mother.

The path of most resistance was to follow the dreams. It was a tremendous leap of faith; I had no idea how to reach those goals. A wise man once said to take it one step at a time. I did know that I could not afford to sit and just let things happen. I had to try to be prepared for anything that might offer an opportunity or even a potential problem. Sure, there were mistakes and bad decisions, but I resolved to be as prepared as possible for whatever happened. My journey to find a better life appeared unlikely at best.

Later in life I had an experience that will serve as an amusing example of attempting to be prepared for any situation. I accepted an invitation from a young lady to attend a formal dinner party which was to be held in her parent's elaborate home. I was one of many guests, but was reluctant to accept because I knew for certain that I was out of my element.

The young lady was very persuasive and so I agreed to be her guest. She assured me that she would help me and a short course in proper etiquette to prepare me was completed before the event. The guests gathered for the grand dinner; I was apprehensive, until I saw the most elegant setting for a meal that I had ever seen, then I was petrified. I whispered to my date that I had never seen so much silverware and glass wear at one place in all of my life. She assured me that everything would be fine. She was going to sit on the opposite side of the table and I was to watch her and whatever she picked up I was to follow suit.

Dinner began and I gained confidence as the evening wore on. I was feeling very comfortable until the meal was nearing its conclusion, and the waiter rolled this large block of ice with red roses on it to the table and stopped, you guessed it, right beside me. I had to do something so I took a red rose and had my face to turn the same hue when the guest next to me placed his fingers on the ice and dried his hands. Memory fails about what happened to the long stem red rose, but I think it may have been given to the young lady as a going away present; so much for being prepared for every eventuality.

A renewed dedication to dreams and restoration of a mother's faith seemed to provide a greater focus to life. I concentrated on my studies in school and resurrected the flame for basketball. The dreams were still alive and some disappointments could not blot out the positive events that were happening.

Grundy High School had no guidance counselors, and any planning of curriculum and courses of study were left to the individual student. I decided that I did not want to be limited in choices that might be necessary for college, so I opted to take the more demanding courses of study. Math and science courses appeared to be the best preparation for college and a definite pattern began to emerge to shape the future.

College remained an ultimate goal (or the unreachable star) while the elements of a plan for fulfilling a mother's hope that her son would graduate from high school were falling into place. I worked diligently on studies and was rewarded with good grades and several achievement awards. I was selected to attend Boys State in Blacksburg on the campus of Virginia Tech. It was the first trip to an institution of higher education and I was overwhelmed. I was also selected to participate in a State forensics competition in which I discovered that facing my own classmates was much different than competing at an event where everyone was a winner. I had an essay on conservation judged to be good enough for second place in a State competition. Sister Ruby would later trump my effort when she was awarded first place for her essay on "What the American Soldier Means to Me."

Dreams of graduating from high school and some ancillary dreams were progressing as well as could be expected and each new day brought exciting opportunities to explore. There was never a day that I did not want to go to school except maybe those days when I was not prepared for a test or an assignment for class. Being in school was a privilege, as I remembered how close I had come to losing that privilege.

It was one of those times when one could have pondered the question "What would life have been like if dropping out of school had been the only option?" Dreams that once appeared to be so unattainable were becoming a reality for me. Dreams do come true, especially if one is willing to put forth the effort to pursue them. Everything was on track to fulfill one of the dreams. Graduation from high school was definitely within reach.

Time is a relentless force and waits for no man. My senior year in high school was a blur with so many activities and exciting events. But wait! What happened to the junior year? Did it just pass into oblivion along with the passion for the dream of playing basketball? Not quite. There were a number of incidents that are worth noting, but are not unique to most students.

Entrance into the junior year in high school was getting close to some major decisions that were pending. It was almost as if it was a holding pattern for the senior year. The academic work was progressing well with the exception of Spanish. It was a requirement for graduation and I had not managed to schedule the class. It was either Spanish or Latin and there was no way that I was going to subject myself to Mr. Glenn's Latin class. So Spanish it was, and with the help of a class mate, I managed to clear the requirement for a Foreign Language.

Staying the course to pursue the dream of playing basketball had not been forgotten. Persistence paid off and I made the Junior Varsity team and played center at five-foot-ten. Draw your own conclusions as to how successful the team was. Still, it was organized and the uniforms were standard equipment; all players wore the blue and gold of the Grundy Golden Wave.

PART TWO

Education

Georgia State Graduation

THE SENIOR YEAR

The summer of 1952 provided time to reflect on the 1952–53 school year. There was no doubt that I was going to graduate come May of 1953. Grades were very good and baring some unforeseen disaster, I was going to accomplish what my mother and I had envisioned five years earlier – graduation from high school! Had it really been five years ago that there was a serious question as to whether or not I was going to even be able to continue to attend school?

I had worked summers and weekends since I was fifteen years old. The first job was working at Vern Elswick's ESSO Service Station which was three miles from home. That was good because I had to walk to and from the station to get to work. It was also fortunate that I had a job since Dad had to care for and support my sisters. Juggling school, basketball, part time work, and helping with chores at home provided for a full schedule. It was especially difficult when friends and classmates stopped at the station for gasoline. They chided me and tried to convince me to leave the station and go with them. However, working was not an option; it was a necessity for survival. That summer was very interesting working at Joe Matney's ESSO Service Station (No it is not a typing error. The name was changed to EXXON much later). I was excited about my senior year and tried to anticipate all that was in store for me.

The dreams to this point were rather simple compared to what faced me as I prepared to enter the final year of high school. I had come a long way, but there were miles to go. The goal of playing basketball had been achieved since I had played on the Junior Varsity squad and would play on the Varsity team in the fall.

The senior year held a few surprises. The election of class officers was the first order of business and much to my surprise I was being nominated for class president. I had not sought the position and was running against Bob Harman who was captain of the football team, an A student, and easily one of the most popular boys in school. In addition, he was my idol. Three ballots resulted in a dead heat each time. It turned out that Bob and I had voted for each other and would not change our vote, but someone else changed their vote and I was the Senior Class President.

Bob held no animosity over the election for President of the Senior Class. He demonstrated his support as classes began in September and everyone knows that is football season. I had never played football and had not intended to subject myself to the rigors of a contact sport as I began the Senior Year. As luck would have it one afternoon I was walking home from school and who should come along but my friend, Bob Harman who was taking an afternoon drive with his girlfriend and they stopped and gave me a ride.

Football practice had already begun and Bob was the quarterback and easily the best player on the team. As they neared my house, the subject came up about the team and their chances this year. It was the first time I had been recruited for any sport and fact is, had always had to market myself for any team. Had the football gods awakened and noticed me? It wasn't likely and I told Bob that I had never played except backyard pickup and was almost always picked last.

Bob was persistent and I finally agreed to come out for the team the following Monday afternoon. One aspect which I liked was the pre- practice that was held the sixth period of the day. It just so happened that the players were excused from classes during the sixth period, which they used to dress for practice and gathering on the playground just outside the classrooms before boarding a school bus that would take them to the football field. Needless to say, the classes adjacent to the school grounds had to compete with the distractions until all members of the team were ready to board the bus. However, it provided players an opportunity to show-off their prowess while waiting for everyone to assemble for the ride to the ball field. It didn't last long because it was time to board the big yellow cheese to ride to the practice field that was seven miles away. Showtime was over and was replaced by the September heat, sand, sun, and infrequent water breaks. Had I somehow made a colossal mistake? I wondered whether Bob was getting back because of the election. Nah.

The football season was a breakeven affair; I even managed to play but not very well. The football coach, Frank Spraker, liked to point out that I weighed a whopping 125 pounds soaking wet. I wouldn't run over many 200 pound linemen, but I did get to play. Dad got to attend one game, but I wasn't fortunate to see action in that particular game. Then came basketball season. One dream had become a reality; just as we ran onto the court for our first varsity game, I couldn't help but remember all those hours that had been devoted to my goal. I earned a letter, bought a school jacket, and promptly allowed a young underclasswoman to wear it the rest of the season.

The senior year at Grundy High was like a rollercoaster with no brakes. The lofty dreams and the idea of reaching for the stars were beginning to demand attention of the highest priority. It was a bittersweet time for me. The dream of graduating from high school was right on target. However, the next rung of the ladder of success was nowhere near the target. Time was running out and there were few alternatives for moving toward the dreams that had appeared to be so simple to formulate earlier. It was simple. The next goal was to get accepted into college. "How; When; Where;" were just some of the questions to which I had no answers.

The selection of a college or university for one's higher education experience should be based on a well-defined plan of action. The plan should be developed after considerable research has been done to answer a number of questions: Where do you want to spend the next four or five years of your life? Are the programs and degrees offered extensive enough to meet your interests? What are the entrance requirements and can you meet them? What is the cost and can you afford it? Is the institution reputable and accredited?

Ordinarily, students had assistance from the school for their plans for the future. However, there were no guidance counselors or programs at Grundy High School to which one could turn for assistance. A few bulletins were available to students in the library, but you had to know enough to ask about them. The ball was in our court when making a decision about college. I had been astute enough to select courses in high school that would not limit choices of colleges. With that exception, I was totally unprepared to pursue one of the most important dreams that Mother and I had discussed. Talk about a step of faith.

All other considerations aside, I had to go somewhere I could afford to go. That certainly was narrowing the scope of the dream. A discussion with a group of friends raised the question about what they would be doing after high school. Several of them had decided what they would do, and the question eventually got around to me. I fumbled around for a politically correct response and one of my friends suggested that I should consider joining them on a trip to the Newport News Shipbuilding Apprentice School in Newport News, Virginia. It just so happened that they had an apprentice program that would pay you to learn a trade. It sounded too good to be true, but further urging by classmates convinced me to accompany them to Tidewater, Virginia.

The trip down to Newport News was interesting since this was all new to me. I had never been this far away from Grundy and I was a bit apprehensive about the new experience. I kept thinking that this was not a college and was getting far from the dream. It was only a site visit and I didn't have to commit, so I could relax and enjoy the experience. The group from Grundy arrived and checked into the school dormitory before reporting to the administration building. The rooms were quite adequate and much more than I had been accustomed to. I was in awe of the size of the operation and felt a little lost. I settled in and received information about the visit to the Apprentice School.

We toured the school, which also included a visit to the area where the ships were being built and repaired. It was a mammoth operation with thousands of people moving about as they performed their responsibilities. The odor in the air caused by joining metal to metal was distinctive and one we would experience again.

The apprenticeship program at the Newport News Shipbuilding and Drydock Company, simply stated, was designed to prepare someone for a trade in the shipbuilding industry. There were openings to become an apprentice for an electrician, plumber, and ship fitter. Training for any of the trades was offered with the idea that upon graduation the individual would choose to be an apprentice for the shipbuilding industry. It was not a requirement, but management hoped students would feel a sense of obligation to remain with the company once they had completed their training.

The most popular choice for a trade was that of electrician. If an apprentice excelled in this training, it was possible to have the opportunity to gain a scholarship to attend college with all expenses paid by the Newport News Shipbuilding and Drydock Company (NNS&DD). Very attractive, but the chances of being selected for this program were also very limited. A prerequisite to be chosen for this honor was to excel as an apprentice in electricity. Other alternatives for formal coursework for college credit were the night courses available that did not interfere with the regular apprentice program.

The dream of going to college was beginning to take on the label of the unreachable star. Representatives of the Atlantic Coast Conference or the Southeastern Conference were not breaking down the doors to offer an invitation to any of their schools. For that matter, no institution of higher education had shown any interest in having me as a student athlete or even as a regular student.

A wise man once said, "Never look a gift horse in the mouth." I didn't know all the ramifications of that statement, but here was another one of those crossroads decisions. Here was an opportunity to learn a trade that would not cost anything except time, and would pay me while I became a master of a trade. Everyone completed application forms for possible acceptance into the apprentice program and left the endless waterways of Tidewater to return to the hills of southwestern Virginia. All the way home, I considered the alternatives before me. Life would change regardless of the path chosen. Had I run out of options? Was harsh reality closing in again to rob me of the opportunity to realize a dream?

Life returned to normal as the novelty of the trip to the outside world became old news. One of the teachers became aware of the trip and wanted to hear about the experience. She asked whether or not we had heard of the program at Virginia Tech that allowed a student to attend classes for a quarter and work a quarter. It was a co-op program with some of the same features of the apprentice school and I did not know of its existence. One exciting difference was that it required matriculation into the university. The possibility of getting into a college or university under any program was cause for joy. Prospective students must be accepted into the university before being considered for the co-op program. Applications were submitted with great anticipation only to learn that many other people were interested in the program. I received a letter from the admissions office informing me that I had been accepted into the regular freshman class, but not for the co-op program. I had researched the cost to attend the university and the last time I had checked the till, it was still empty.

One other possibility for a chance to be accepted into a college or university came from the history teacher at Grundy. She and her husband had come to Grundy from a small junior college in North Georgia and they were willing to help me gain entrance into that institution. Young Harris Junior College was willing to accept me into the freshman class. Little did I know that I could have been hobnobbing with a future governor of Georgia; Zell Miller and I could have shared a legacy as graduates of Young Harris. Unfortunately, even with scholarships and grants, some money was required and I had none.

Graduation came for the Class of 1953 on the night of May twenty-sixth. It was a time of celebration, a time of introspection, and a time to reflect on what the future might hold. The class was reminded that graduation was not an end in itself, but a means to an end. It was the first step of the rest of our lives. The questions of *how*, *when*, and *where*, still had to be reconciled. Meanwhile, I knew Mother was smiling all the way from heaven to the stage of that auditorium as I took the last steps to reach the summit of the mountain and claim a dream.

SPECIAL NIGHT

I couldn't help thinking how close I had been to assuming my rightful place as a coal miner, married to one of my high school girlfriends, and struggling to provide a life for family on the strength of an eighth grade education. I remember what Mother had said to me when we talked about our mutual dream, "You will never set foot in a coal mine if it is in my power to prevent it." It seemed that even in her untimely death, she would not accept the stereotype existence of her son as a coal miner. I never worked a day in the mines even though it had been a close call.

The night of the twenty-sixth was special because it was not just a high school graduation, but it was the culmination of a part of a dream that was seemingly an impossible sojourn to an unreachable star. I was moved to share the realization of a dream with classmates at the fifty-fifth reunion of the Class of 1953. This vignette was included to honor that unique group of individuals. The short story is included as it was written on the eve of a special night:

"Someone has speculated that we cannot ignore the past unless we are prepared to repeat it. It has been speculated that one cannot escape the past, nor ignore the lessons of history unless they are ready to face the same experiences and the same consequences over and over. Perhaps that is a true statement, but one shouldn't be too sure that the past can be ignored at any cost. To deny the past is to deny identity – after all, one is the sum total of all experiences good, bad, and indifferent. As individuals or groups of individuals who share a common bond, the class is known not so much for what has been experienced, but for how they responded to those experiences and how they changed us and made us who we are. I prefer to have it said of the class, 'we were not the first by which the new was tried, nor yet the last by which the old is put aside.' We never spoke too soon, but after careful consideration of the facts, rendered the decisions which allowed us to reach for the stars and pursue the impossible dream.

We are the sons and daughters of parents whose ancestors from various backgrounds found their way into the ruggedly, beautiful mountains of Buchanan County, Virginia. They settled the land and we shared

James H. Stiltner

a heritage that had been determined for us. We grew up in a culture that was influenced greatly by the presence of 'blackgold,' better known as coal. The precious resources that had been stored up for millions of years in the mountains of southwest Virginia would prove to be lucrative for some and a hard taskmaster for others. At any rate, there is no doubt that coal was the major factor that helped to shape a culture that would provide a proving ground to test the mettle of the class and distinguish them as individuals and as a unique group.

The coal mining industry affected everyone, and this environment provided experiences that would shape an identity and determine who and what we would become. We were influenced by the fact that we were situated in a rural setting geographically. Even though most of us were from the town of Grundy, by no stretch of the imagination could we be called 'urbanites.' While we enjoyed some of the elements of urbanization and neighboring communities like Garden, Hurley, and Whitewood, often referred to us as 'city folks,' the fact remains that the closest metropolitan areas were the twin cities of Bluefield, Virginia/ West Virginia and Bristol, Virginia/ Tennessee.

Several other factors influenced lives as we grew in knowledge and awareness of surroundings that would help us to become responsible citizens. We learned to cope with criticism and ridicule leveled by people outside the community suggesting we might

107

just be rednecks because the grass in the front yard was brown where the refrigerator had been sitting (shades of Jeff Foxworthy). True, we grew up in a small, rural, isolated mining part of the state of Virginia, but a cross section of this little part of the world revealed we were not so different from people in other parts of the country. In fact, there were advantages to be enjoyed that were not available in other places.

The class grew from children into young adults in a culture that was clouded with so many memories. It can be recalled that the worst transgression was chewing gum in school. The only thing worse was getting caught and losing free period that had to be used to scrape the gum off the floor and the desks. This is not to suggest that some did not get into trouble on occasion, because we did.

However, compared to today's challenges to young people, we were fortunate, indeed, to grow into young adults in an environment of love and concern provided by parents, teachers, neighbors, the comm.-unity, and God. Does one dare suggest that as individuals and a particular group we were better than other students in this little corner of the world, or, for that matter, students all over the world? Not at all! However, they did have a few things going such as the phenomenon of what is referred to as selective memory. As one grows older, they tend to remember the good times and shut out the bad. We may even embellish the memories from time to time. 'Ah, we remember it well.'

Lest one forget, there was a very important element that helped to determine the uniqueness of the class. Some would say that to be isolated didn't necessarily mean disadvantaged. We sensed just the opposite. There was a sense of pride that was shared for Grundy High School, the small town, the teachers, parents, and the community. Faith and trust in God strengthened the resolve to be the best.

Was the class unique? Selective memory suggests we were, parents thought we were, and most of the teachers found something unique in everyone. And, yes, if a vote was taken the class alphabetically from Larry 'Hop' Akers to Bill Yates would probably agree as Yogi Bear would say, 'we're smarter than the average bear.'

However, it did take an extra year to graduate. While members of the class were studying diligently to get out of elementary school and into high school, the powers in Richmond and other state governments decided to add another grade to help make the transition from elementary school to high school. We had the distinction of being the first class to graduate from Grundy High School with a transcript indicating we completed seven years of elementary school and five years of high school. Transition or not, it still seemed like high school. Did the extra year make us smarter and help transition to high school easier? Who can say?

Matriculation into high school opened new vistas and the enrollment grew slightly. With the exception of a few who moved away and a few who moved in to join the class, an identity was established. We claimed the distinction that would bind us together forever when we walked across the stage on that balmy May 26th night to receive diplomas from Principal John Meade and become a member of the Grundy High School Graduation Class of 1953. It is a distinction that we will never lose.

We were 103 strong by the time all exams were completed and grades recorded. It was reported there were 104 members of the graduating class, but a copy of the 1953 Pioneer contains only 103 smiling faces. The yearbook was edited by a committee under the capable guidance of the Journalism Club. What came of the poor lost soul who caused the discrepancy between 103 and 104? 'Only the Shadow Knows.'

Just as quickly as the years seemed to fly by and as we had bonded with our classmates, we departed from that memorable May 26th evening and went our separate ways. It was said of our class that we had one of the highest percentages of students to pursue some form of higher education or specialized training. I can't vouch for that statistic because my research is woefully lacking. I do know that our class produced some impressive contributions in a variety of vocations and avocations. The class members would make their marks in medicine, dentistry, business and industry, engineering, public service, the legal profession, education, banking, social work and religion, to name a few.

Our class had its share of entrepreneurs, especially in the coal industry. Some became wealthy and others 'owed their souls to the company store.' Those who did well had to have a place to keep their hard-earned cash, so some of our class built a bank to keep what was left after the IRS took its share. Some would go away to school to learn how to account for our assets, large or small. For those of us who didn't have to worry about vast resources, the bank extended credit so we could pursue the impossible dream. However, as we continued to learn and evolve into a unique group with an identity, we came to realize that we had much for which to be grateful. Selective memories, notwithstanding, there is much to be said about the opportunity to grow up in a free country and be able to dream and have many of those dreams come true. We have 'come home again' even if it is only in our dreams. A quick look back allows us to test our selective memory.

It was fifty-five years ago that we left the safe, secure and comfortable environment we knew as the land of the Golden Wave. We can recall the game of 'whip crack' where we would hold hands and form a long line that started slowly, but gained momentum quickly. One of our daredevil young ladies wanted to be at the end of the whip and wanted me to hold on to her because I wouldn't let go. It was great fun until the day the whip was the longest ever tried, and you guessed it...the speed was so great that the grip gave way and Jean got the worst of it. Sorry Jean.

I can recall the intramural basketball games played at noon between the grades and home rooms. It was also great to get out of class to see the boys and girls basketball games with other schools. Remember the girls played half court because they, supposedly, were not as strong as the boys and they could dribble only twice before passing the ball. The guards could not go past mid court nor shoot the ball and the forwards could shoot the ball but could not go past mid court either. I do not know what the center did, but perhaps some of the class could refresh us.

Then there was the ritual of Friday night football. Bob Harman and Bill Rowe led us against such formidable foes as the Richlands Blue Tornado, the Green Dragons of Garden, the Hurley Rebels, the Virginia Bearcats, and other less ferocious sounding opponents as Tazewell, Graham, Abingdon, and Lebanon. We were cheered on by the winsome cheerleaders who also cheered for our Boys Basketball Team which was in a building year. Were we unique as a basketball team? Well, at five-feet-ten-inches, weighing in at 125 pounds wringing wet, I was back–up to the center who was barely six feet tall. The verdict is still out, at least on the strength of our selective memories.

The class of 1953 was involved in more than extra-curricular activities. Our time was spent studying, attending class, and honing academic skills that would lead us along the yellow brick road. I have committed an unpardonable error by naming a few classmates and their accomplishments while I am not able to do the same for everyone. Hopefully, we can use the few examples to help us realize that as a part of our unique group we each share in the gains, loses, successes, failures, etc. attributable to the group.

If one of us dies, a part of the group dies as does a part of each one of us. If one of us is successful, we all share in that sense of accomplishment. How so, you ask? Allow me to give a 'for instance:' One of our own became a successful teacher and when someone asks about him, the response could easily be, 'You know him, he is a part of the 1953 Graduation Class of Grundy High School.' We all feel a kinship and share in the success of people like Bob Harman and Lee Hess who were successful dentists. I knew them, they were part of the 1953 graduating at Grundy and it was my privilege to be a part of that class. We share a common bond that will never be broken. It would be interesting to enumerate the accomplishments of all the members of the class, but time and space does not permit. However, we can be proud that we made a difference both as individuals and as a group with a common bond.

Upon graduation, we went our separate ways to make our mark in the world. We came together on three other class reunions, before scheduling one for celebrating the fifty-fifth one for September 13, 2008. We anticipate this will be the final organized event for us unless someone discovers the fountain of youth. So there should be something to mark this event with a culminating statement that helps to preserve the past through our selective memories, embrace the present, and anticipate the changes that are inevitable in the future. I made the suggestion to our class coordinators who were organizing the event and they were in agreement that something should be written. They also indicated I should do the writing. I should have known better than to make the suggestion, but I am not one of 'you're smarter than the average bear' guys, so you will get what you pay for.

There was not much change for the first several years after graduation, except we knew fewer and fewer people when we visited. Not much changed in the town of Grundy except coal production declined, the population declined, and the economy spiraled downward. It became so bad that property values dropped to the point that one couldn't give land away. Exodus from the county suggested that the town might dry up and blow away. It appeared that conditions could not offer much hope for the future. Sometimes the night is darkest just before dawn, but then the darkness clears and then there is a silver lining that pushes the doom and gloom away. Could there be a silver lining that would not be ignored and tossed on the 'what if' heap? It could be, and there were some diehard residents who were not ready to throw in the towel. Perhaps I have been away too long to tell, but I sensed a change in the attitude and determination of some key individuals who were ready and willing to work for change. Progress was slow, but gathered momentum as more and more doubting Thomas's joined the diehard visionaries.

Evidence of this new attitude and vision can be cited in several areas. A landmark event was the establishment of a regional law school. Critics said it would never make it, said the school would never become accredited, and no one would come to Grundy to go to law school. They were wrong on all accounts. The Appalachian School of Law is established and housed in our old school which has been renovated. If you haven't seen it, take the advice of a television personality named 'Randy' and 'Check it out.' The school is fully accredited and I understand that people come from all parts of the country to attend the law school.

Other evidence of change includes the new School of Pharmacy and the establishment of a Law School Library. These new organizations and establishments create a need for support services, small businesses, and human resources. Land and property that had previously declined in value is enjoying resurgence and is much in demand. These are positive signs of growth and progress that in a few years will not resemble the Grundy that we knew. Our 'old school' has been regenerated and has new life. Likewise the 'old town of Grundy' and the county are changing. You've heard the saying, 'faith can move mountains.' They are literally moving a mountain of rock to relocate the 'New Grundy.' Our town and our school will never be the same. Earlier we quoted Thomas Wolfe who said you can't go back home. We disagreed and contended we could go back home even if it were in our selected memories. However, it becomes more and more difficult to hold on to our selected memories as we grow older and things change around us. Memories are precious and we must hold onto them, but we must always analyze and integrate the changes that are making new memories which, hopefully, will keep us young as we step boldly into the future.

Members of the Grundy High School Graduating Class of 1953, we were destined to be a part of this unique group to make our mark in this world. We made that mark and we did it our way.

Hopefully, we will continue to expand on that mark as we enjoy reminiscing and looking forward to tomorrow. Class of 1953 we have been blessed and to us much has been given so much is demanded of us. This is not our swan song, rather, it is our opportunity to protect selected memories, live in the present as if it were our last day, and embrace the future as it unfolds before us. It is a pleasure to be part of this unique group."

Old Grundy

New Grundy

A JOURNEY TO REMEMBER

The dream of going to college appeared to be one of those unreachable stars, but not all was lost. I received notice that I had been accepted into the Apprentice School at Newport News and my trade would be ship fitter. It was not even the choice of trades to pursue, but the price was right. I took the hand that was dealt and went about finding a way to Newport News.

The Newport News experience began much as one would expect. The first objective was to become acquainted with a work schedule and life in general. I found the gym and learned there was a team that participated in what amounted to a limited non- league program. The gym was my venue for reducing stress. I also learned that my first responsibility was to learn to weld. If I was to fit large pieces of metal to the sides of a ship, welding was definitely a prerequisite. It also reminded me that learning to be a welder might offer vocational choices other than fitting metal to the sides of large ships. The learning curve was steep and there was little room for error and not much patience from regularly employed workers. Stay out of the way, obey the rules, and do your job. One of those rules came as a surprise when I realized there were separate facilities for blacks and whites. Drinking fountains, as well as bathroom facilities, were marked, "For blacks only" and "For whites only."

My first encounter with racial discrimination was when I attempted to get a drink of water; someone pointed to the sign above the water fountain. I was about to commit the unpardonable sin of drinking from the water fountain that was for blacks only. No black people resided in Buchanan County and the only exposure that I had had was through the television programs. To say that I had led a sheltered life would be an understatement. The cold, cruel world waited.

Life settled into a routine. Breakfast time came early followed by prompt attendance at the work stations. The work station contained a pair of welding gloves, a welding mask, and pieces of metal to be welded together using the tools of the trade. The supervisor explained techniques and proper procedures to be utilized to join one piece of metal to another. It looked simple enough, but was I ever wrong. A few clumsy attempts indicated I was in for a lot of practice. The supervisor was a master welder and his hands moved like a surgeon as he patiently demonstrated proper techniques and procedures for bonding metal to metal. Would I ever master this art?

Training was rigorous, but time was scheduled for rest and relaxation. Most of the free time was spent in the gym and on the bunk bed in the dorm reflecting on the status of dreams to go to college. Class work in subjects related to our trade was definitely not my idea of a college experience. I was not a happy camper, and after two weeks was ready to give up on something. It did not occur to me that it wasn't giving up as much as it was reestablishing the original dream. Colleagues from Grundy who had been accepted into the program tried to persuade me to stay. They reminded me that it would take money to go to college and the school year had begun two weeks ago. My mind was made up and I collected my belongings and hit the road.

The journey from Newport News to Grundy was a long one and as it turned out, a very interesting one. I had not been paid and there were no credit cards that could be used to pay the bus fare. A quick check revealed that my resources included a few dollars and some change. Most of the money paid for a ticket to get out of town, but it wasn't enough to go all the way to Grundy. I recalled that the bus ride lasted through the night and daybreak found me in Bluefield, Virginia. The remainder of the trip would have to be navigated by hitchhiking, a mode of travel I did not relish. I didn't like asking for rides from strangers, but there were no other alternatives.

Bluefield is a twin city located partly in Virginia and partly in West Virginia. It had a reputation as the air-conditioned city and it comes by the name honestly. It was not uncommon to wake up to an early frost in late September. It was one of those mornings, and I was not anxious to leave the warm environs of the bus depot. It was also time to reflect upon what had become a sad state of affairs for someone who was considered to be in command of most of his faculties. I had just left an opportunity to train as an apprentice of a master welder and was being paid for the effort. Here I sat with no money, no plan, and no one to turn to for help; dreams do not always come true and the unreachable star is really unreachable.

The time for meditation was over and it was time to begin the next leg of the journey to Grundy. Just as I prepared to trust the goodness and kindness of the people in Bluefield by asking for a ride with anyone going my way, it occurred to me that I did know someone who lived in this town. Jimmy Statzer was a young man who aspired to be a preacher. He had led a revival in the Grundy Baptist Church the past spring and had become romantically involved with Joyce Davis, who was a friend. I remembered that he had said he was a student at Bluefield College and would be studying for the ministry.

A decision was made to delay departure for home and try to locate Jimmy. He was in school in the air-conditioned city and he also lived here. It was relatively easy to find him in the telephone book and he was at home when I called. He was happy to hear from me and asked if I would be interested in visiting for a while. I was interested, and was picked up at the bus station. We talked about how I happened to be in town.

I had confided that the reason for leaving the Apprentice School was that it was not a college program. Jimmy suggested that I might want to consider the possibility of attending Bluefield College. It was a Baptist supported institution and since I was a Baptist they would be sensitive to my needs. My mind began to race as I wondered whether or not this was a door of opportunity that had opened.

Bluefield College was a small two-year Baptist institution whose mission was to give students a basic academic foundation with emphasis on religion. I knew nothing about it, but there was little time to consider all the pros and cons so I accepted a ride to the campus for a possible date with destiny. People in the Admissions Office were most kind and helpful and I found myself in the process of making an application for admittance to the school.

I was accepted into the freshman class of a college that five hours ago I didn't know existed. Acceptance was pending receipt of high school transcripts and the payment of tuition and fees. We explored the available scholarships and other financial assistance for which I was eligible, but at least five hundred dollars more per semester was needed. I registered and attended two classes that morning then left for Grundy to find enough money to close the deal.

Hitchhiking is an interesting way to travel. It can be dangerous, but it's cheap. Depending on whether or not the person offering the ride is talkative, it can be a time to reflect on many things, like "am I dreaming or is this really happening to me?" I had always been the talkative one.

The tone of the conversation determines whether or not one wishes to get out at the next milepost. Fortunately, I had to abort the ride only one or two times in all experiences. One disadvantage to this mode of travel is that one may have to change rides several times to reach the desired destination.

Maybe Lady Luck was riding with me on this day, for it took a minimum of rides to arrive at home. Actually, I did not go home and the people who stopped to give me a ride were not all that eager to learn about my life history. That was good, because it gave me time to think about how to convince someone that it would be a prudent move to loan a teenager five hundred dollars. I did not want to go home and have to tell Dad what I had done and what I was trying to do.

I was so absorbed in the task at hand that I appeared to be wandering aimlessly around the small town. It did not take long to realize that very few people had five hundred dollars to spare and fewer still who might consider making an unsecured loan. I was beginning to feel a sense of defeat and beginning to wonder whether mother and I had set our sights too high. This mountain was too high to climb. Ignorance of what is required to matriculate into an institution of higher education was probably the most damaging limitation to the goal. Blind faith would not get the job done. "The night is darkest just before dawn," is a saying that may or may not be based on fact. The darkness was closing on this dream and it did not appear to have a silver lining. Indulging in a private pity party, I was unaware that my aimless wandering had brought me to the entrance of the high school. I never ceased to be impressed by the beauty of the school that was built in the WPA days. The school day was over and the students had departed for home, but the front door was still open. I could see that the principal, Mr. John Meade, was in his office so I decided to say hello.

We visited and he asked what I had been up to since graduation. I said it was a long story and Mr. Meade said, "I have time." I recounted the time spent at the Apprentice School, the decision to leave and the events of the last several hours, including unsuccessful attempts to raise the money to attend Bluefield College. He asked about my plans for the remainder of the afternoon and evening, and when he learned there were no plans he invited me to be his guest at the Rotary Club for their dinner meeting. He informed me that the Rotary Club maintained a student loan fund to help students. The invitation was accepted without hesitation.

Mr. Meade did not know how much money was available in the fund and what the conditions were for getting a loan. Could it be that the dawn might have a silver lining after all? In the interim as we waited to go to the meeting, the conversation was about a recent visit he had with a representative from a college in Bristol, Tennessee. It appeared that someone from King College had discussed the possibility of accepting a young woman or young man from the Grundy area into the freshman class at King. I had never heard of the college and was informed that it was a small Presbyterian college interested in establishing a contact in the area. Scholarships and workshops were available and five hundred dollars would cover expenses for two semesters. The five hundred dollar figure appeared to take on a life of its own.

The Rotarians assembled and the meeting began with a delicious dinner for which I was most grateful since it had been a very full day. Several very successful and affluent business men were members of the Rotary and I knew of them only by reputation. It was the first time I had faced such a group of influential people whose decision might change my life. The agenda for the business session was amended to include a request from Mr. Meade. The request was to consider making a loan to a young man for the purpose of attending college. He presented a good justification on my behalf, including what had transpired in Bluefield and the offer that had been extended from King College.

A short break was called to allow time to consider the request. The meeting was resumed and the Scholarship Committee brought in their recommendation. As it turned out, they did not loan money, but instead awarded scholarships that did not have to be repaid. I was awarded the scholarship which was limited to, you guessed it, five hundred dollars. The scholarship could be used at any college or university. Outside, night had descended, the silver lining began to appear and the dream was still alive. I reflected later on the events of this day and marveled at the "coincidences" I had encountered in a twenty-four hour period. Any number of times I could have been forgiven if I had called a halt and declared enough is enough. Could that many coincidences happen at just the precise moment, or were God's angels directing my path on that day? I knew I was definitely not in control, for there was no way I could have orchestrated those events.

Wait, there was more. There were still some unresolved issues; Mr. Meade wanted to know where I was going to school. I had given some thought to that question and decided that five hundred dollars would pay for two semesters at King College whereas it would pay for only one semester at Bluefield. Talk about a leap of faith! I stopped to reflect, I had withdrawn from an institution that assured me of learning a trade and a way to achieve it, had applied for and been accepted as a student at one college that I had not heard of before that day, decided I would not attend that institution, made a decision to attend another college I had never heard of before that day either, expected to be accepted for classes that had been in session for more than two weeks, assumed that I could pass the entrance exams, and expected the admissions office was ready to welcome me with open arms.

There was still the matter of getting to King College so this grand scheme could unfold. My principal knew the answer before I asked, but he wanted to know how I planned to get to Bristol, Tennessee. My response was that I did not know, whereupon, I was instructed to go home to leave at seven o'clock in the morning for Bristol.

I didn't want to even attempt to explain how to enlighten the family on all that had been happening. That is a story in itself. I was ready at seven and we left for the one hundred mile trip with the promise of a five hundred dollar scholarship and an invitation to make an application for acceptance to King College. Not only was my principal taking a day to transport me to a possible college experience, he made some visits after leaving the meeting to collect three pairs of dress trousers and two sport jackets to complement my wardrobe. The benefactor was a classmate who was roughly the same size as I was. Mr. Meade knew that I would have need of more than a few pairs of Levi's, and he suspected that this show of generosity would avoid some embarrassing moments for me.

We arrived at the college, found the Admissions Office and announced our intentions. Once again the sojourn was explained with my principal filling in the background. An entrance exam was administered, and an application for admission to King College was completed. The school officials were impressed with some aspect of my background and experiences or they were desperate to have a representative at the college from the southwestern part of the state of Virginia. I was accepted to the Freshman Class of 1953 and was informed that there was one bed left in the dormitory. A student had decided that he had enough of college life at King and he was moving out. He moved out as I moved in; I could hardly believe the whirlwind of activities that had helped to reach for that unreachable star and restore a dream. Mr. Meade left for the return trip to Grundy after he was assured that I was properly situated. He was a guardian angel that will never be forgotten. Of all the people who had entered my life, Principal John Meade was the one most responsible for whatever success I had or ever will have. Had he not been working late that day, or willing to interrupt his after school plans, or to listen to the problems of one of his former students, life would have been decidedly different.

I am eternally grateful for his willingness to go far above and beyond the call of duty to help me achieve a very important goal. God was intervening in my life and Mr. Meade was one of the instruments He was using to direct my steps. The ball was squarely in my court since I was now a student at a four year college with a renewed goal of earning a college degree. My journey had been filled with problems, frustrations, and mistakes, but with the help of a lot of people, not the least of which was my high school principal, the top of the mountain was clearly in sight.

I stood in the center of the basement in Anderson Hall that had been converted to a dormitory room and paused to reflect on what was in store. My two roommates, one of whom was Dillard "Zeke" Keen, shared bunk beds and since I was late in arriving, the top bunk bed belonged to me. Zeke figured prominently in my future and would marry Cousin Lillian. It is another story that should be told.

Perhaps it was not exactly what I envisioned as a college experience, but I soon learned that King offered a rigorous academic program that was recognized as one of the best in the country. If the goal was to be achieved, it would take a supreme effort to succeed in this highly academic institution of learning. The King College experience was real and by the grace of God an unreachable star had become reachable.

The twenty-four hour period that had begun in the evening at the Newport News Apprentice School in Newport News, Virginia had been an unbelievable sojourn and would live in memory as long as I lived. The decisions and choices that were made changed my life and would affect the lives of thousands of people. If any one of these decisions or choices had been different, the results would have changed not only my life, but the lives of everyone I touched. What if, for example, Mr. Meade had not had time to talk and the trip to Bristol and King College had never taken place? What if the path chosen not been the "one less travelled by?" It would have been much easier to say it is not possible to go to college. However, it did happen just as I said, and all those life changing conditions made all the difference.

Principal John Meade Welcomes Brian to the World.

AM I MY BROTHER'S KEEPER?

I was a work in progress during the college experience and the raw material left something to be desired. The years of having to make decisions and exhibiting an air of confidence that was not always warranted left some with the impression that I had a chip on my shoulder. Confidence in myself that had built up over the years would not allow me to give up on something just because it was difficult. Learning to deal with that attitude was a valuable tool for coping with the life that the King College experience provided. College life took the "attitude" and molded it into a positive approach to problem solving that matched dreams with reality. A quiet demeanor and the ability to be a good listener are positive traits that had been developed and utilized to good advantage.

King College was a fascinating place. It was a small liberal arts college enrolling approximately 360 students, many of whom lived on campus. The composition of the student body was divided almost equally between boys and girls, and more than half of them planned to go into the ministry or some similar vocation.

The college was affiliated with the Presbyterian Church and was considered to be rather conservative. Students were expected to attend devotional service in the Chapel at midmorning each day except Friday and to attend church services each Sunday. Young ladies were required to "dress up" for Sunday dinner and wear hats, and young men were expected to wear a suit and tie or sport coat and dress slacks. I was fortunate to have had a caring and perceptive high school principal who had helped me obtain some dress clothes when I came to King. The composition of the student body suggests that it was a kind and caring place. That was a correct assumption and it was exhibited in many instances. I experienced that genuine concern most notably on three different occasions.

I played on the tennis team and enjoyed competing at the sixth position on the tennis ladder. On this particular day, King was hosting East Tennessee State University. Unfortunately, I was just recuperating from the flu and was not scheduled to participate. I was observing the match as a spectator. As the teams were warming up, I spotted my tennis coach making way toward me. Dr. Ed Burke was the tennis coach as well as the Physics professor. He asked how

I felt and my response was that I was o.k. just a bit weak. "Do you feel well enough to play in a match?" It turned out that two of the members of the team had left early for spring break and the match would be forfeit unless another team member could play. I agreed to give it a try, got dressed and the match began.

It was a hot day and the match was played on concrete courts which quickly sapped my strength. The first few games looked like a tennis match, but the first set was nearly over and I had not won a game. My arms felt as if they were playing one kind of a game and the rest of my body was playing some other game. By the middle of the second set my legs became rubbery and the ball was stroking the racket rather than the racket stroking the ball. The match was over and I had lost 6-0, 6-0.

The world was spinning as the match ended none too soon. I crumpled to the concrete and the next thing I remembered was being extremely thirsty. I could not move my legs or arms and realized I was in a hospital. "A near heat stroke" was the prognosis and the night was spent in Bristol Memorial Hospital. The hospital released me the next day and I was transferred to the King College Infirmary where I spent the next week. Time lost for class work was almost two weeks. Midterm exams were fast approaching and I was in danger of losing a semester of credit.

The one subject that was in most peril was Organic Chemistry. I was worried that I had missed so much time that I wasn't sure that I could pass the exam. I went to see Dr. Roy Bailey who was the

Chemistry professor and shared concerns about missing so much class time and the possibility that I might not be ready for the exams. Dr. Bailey indicated that I should not be concerned because they would spend the weekend covering the material and preparing for the exam. Without the help of another caring individual in my life and the willingness to go the extra mile for one of his students, a precious amount of time would have been lost.

The second illustration of a caring fraternity of people which was very touching but inconspicuous to others, involved an act by an anonymous individual whose identity remains a mystery. I needed to be careful not to appear ungrateful since I could be labeled as someone who was pleading starvation with a loaf of bread under his arm. After all, I had a roof over my head, three meals a day, and a bed to sleep in so what was the problem?

It was a small thing, but the snack bar where everyone headed for a break at nine each night was located on the basement floor of Anderson Hall, the men's dorm. It was before Krispy Kreme doughnuts, but they had the best fresh doughnuts to be found anywhere. It wasn't just the doughnuts and frosty coke, but it was the spot where anyone who was anyone gathered each evening to socialize and be seen. The problem was that I did not have the price of a coke in my pocket and my response to an invitation to join them was that I needed to study.

I was not without money all of the time, but there were weeks when I was without a dime. It was one of those times when my pockets were empty that I went to check the mail boxes. The post office was located in the John F.

Hay Building and the boxes were checked religiously. On this particular day there was a plain white envelope in my box. When I opened it there was a twenty dollar bill inside. I was surprised and wondered who knew just how broke I was. I accused my roommate Charles Owens, but he denied that it was his doing. If it was not Charlie, then who? The only other person that could have been the good Samaritan was my friend in the Business office, Dr. Jack Snider. He said that I must have an admirer, but it was not he. My benefactor was never discovered and I stretched that twenty dollar bill like it was the last one in the universe. Insignificant act you say; not to me it wasn't.

Another insignificant act that didn't go unnoticed or unappreciated involved my good friend Kenneth Phillips. He lived in Bristol and was a day student. Ken and I came to know each other on the basketball court. We both played basketball for King and became good friends almost immediately.

It was one of those Saturday nights when almost everyone was doing anything other than studying. I was in my room pretending to be concentrating mightily with most everything going in one ear and out the other with no stops in between. Suddenly, the door burst open (Ken never went anywhere quietly) and he demanded to know what I was doing on a weekend when everyone else was out enjoying themselves. I tried a lame excuse which Ken summarily dismissed.

He ordered me to get dressed and pack a few necessities for overnight. I was going to spend the night, have breakfast the next morning and spend an enjoyable Sunday before getting back to the grind on Monday. Ken lived in his own apartment and it was just the break that was needed.

These and other acts of kindness were the rule rather than the exception with this community of classmates. I couldn't even get angry with them and if I did, I could not stay angry. How does one reside in such an environment without being influenced and, yes, changed dramatically? On more than one occasion notes were found in my mailbox indicating that gifts of twenty, thirty or fifty dollars had been placed in the box. Never has one owed so much to so many. Little things mean a lot.

I gained a great deal more than a base of knowledge while at King College. An education is so much more than amassing credits for graduation. It is broadening your perspective of the world and developing the ability to make decisions that make a difference. It is a ticket to wonders of life and it allows you to be all that you can become. Do you dare to dream and reach for the unreachable star? We are obligated to be the very best we can be.

THE DREAM IS ALIVE, BUT COLLEGE IS NO PICNIC

College life was a new experience; "apprehensive" is not nearly adequate enough to describe what had happened when the dream dust was swept away by the cold hard facts of reality. What to do now? Classes were assigned which had been in session for two weeks and freshman orientation was a thing of the past. Two weeks of lost class time in high school was one thing, but it would be difficult to make up that much time in college. The tardy student was introduced to twenty or thirty classmates, and it is not certain whether or not they were happy to have someone join them at this late date, but a young lady in the seat next to me smiled and whispered that they would help me catch up. The professor looked at the admission slip and struggled with the name and decided it would be shortened to Jim. So be it. I was here in the hallowed halls of higher education and christened "Jim." Let the trials begin.

I had hardly settled before being informed that the next week was "Rat Week." It was supposed to help freshmen forget their prior awards and recognitions of high school and realize that they were at the lowest level of a new pecking order. Everyone was at the same level and had to earn recognition by their accomplishments in a new arena regardless of what they had done in high school. In reality, it was hazing of freshmen by the upperclassmen. We were at the beck and call of upperclassmen and had to perform acts that presumably were designed to help us to forget the past and focus on the future. Someone offered advice on how to cope with the wild escapades that were happening, so I hid out as much as possible in the dorm room and in the gymnasium. It was an old gym, but well maintained and it had that unmistakable odor that can only come from sweat generated by hours of practice and conditioning. I loved it!

King College was small school but had competitive sports teams in basketball, baseball, and tennis that competed with schools like Carson Newman, Emory and Henry, Lincoln Memorial, Bluefield, Tusculum, Milligan, and Roanoke. On special nights, freshmen teams from the University of Tennessee and East Tennessee State University used our teams as mincemeat. There were no scholarships for student athletes, so participation on the teams was for individuals who were truly dedicated. It also meant that there was fierce competition for a spot on the team. Did I dare think there was a possibility that I might, just might, be able to play for the King College Tornado Basketball Team?

I had persevered in high school and had managed to make the team as a senior. I was still only five feet eleven inches tall and weighed only 125 pounds. Was it possible to expand the dream to include playing basketball at the college level? I would not know unless I gave it a high priority. Basketball season was a couple of months away; there was time to establish myself as a contender. The awards and letters earned at Grundy High School were tucked away, and a new focus was established for performance on a level playing field.

College life at King was new and exciting, but it was no bowl of cherries. Balancing and managing time for work on campus (due to a work study scholarship) raking leaves, for meeting classes, for study, and for basketball practice was a new experience. Social life on campus also demanded some time. The twenty-five dollars borrowed from my barber friend, Claude Davis, and the few dollars Dad had given me were long since gone. The clothes Mr. Meade had collected were a godsend and allowed me to mix socially without embarrassment. Financial arrangements with the Financial Aid Office assured me of tuition, room, and board; there was a roof over my head, a place to sleep and three meals a day. The five hundred dollars from the Rotary Club had bought a bargain, but I suspected some work behind the scenes was done on my behalf. The social life on campus suffered, but hey, I needed only to count my blessings.

The most difficult problem occurred when basketball practice began. Practice sessions were strenuous and tiring and many evenings players left the gym so tired they could hardly walk. We came to realize the cost of a commitment to play at the college level was much higher than expected. We fought the urge to skip dinner and just go to bed but knew that the temptation had to be resisted because to yield to it would mean neglecting other things, such as homework assignments. Conditioning and practice soon became bearable and the routine was established. We could survive after all.

Freshmen were not allowed to play a varsity sport in those days so we had to be content with practicing with the Varsity and playing scrimmage games and a freshman schedule when possible. The maximum number of players that could be carried on the freshman team was twelve. They had one year to sharpen their skills and learn the system before the big moment arrived. Arrive it did and the fun and games were replaced by a serious resolve to make the team. It was a joy and an honor to have the opportunity to compete for a position on the team.

The level of intensity grew as the time approached to determine the composition of the team. Coach Grant Johnson pushed us like there was no tomorrow and finally the axe fell. The names of those who made the roster were posted on the gymnasium bulletin board. There was some question as to whether or not my heart would stand the pressure as I made my way to the gym. It truly was one of the most stressful times I had ever experienced. The list had my name on it and the joy was almost unbearable. I had been chosen to play for the King College Tornado Basketball Team! I had dared to reach for the star and lo and behold I had caught one. Team members enjoyed benefits other than the recognition of being on the team. A training table was set for the team for each meal with a young lady as their exclusive waitress. She was a student, and her work scholarship was to make certain the team was well fed. She ruled with an iron hand and it wasn't good to cross her. Players also had trainers to wrap their ankles for each game and to attend to minor sprains and injuries. Conditioning was crucial to performance but keeping fit was not something that could be taken for granted. Breaking training rules even at this level of competition could end a career in basketball.

There was no trouble with this aspect of the game or regulations of the college. I had worked too hard and sacrificed too much to let anything spoil the dreams for which I had dedicated much of my life. If that was not enough incentive, I had only to remember all the help I had from so many friends and the people who had made it possible to reach this point in my life. That didn't mean I was not discouraged at times, but it didn't take long to regain focus and get back on track to continue the search for the "Holy Grail." At that time I was not certain I understood the concept of the Holy Grail, but hey, that was one of the reasons I went to college...to become educated. Perseverance, hard work, and the will to win helped to move me toward accomplishments that may well have appeared unattainable, but may also have brought me to the very brink of the crossroads to success.

The night of the first game finally arrived; words cannot describe the feelings and emotions of team members when we sprinted onto the court to be introduced. I could not believe I was realizing a dream come true. Memories flooded back to me as I recalled the hours spent fantasizing and pretending I was playing basketball. I also recalled using equipment and hand-me-down uniforms that might suggest I was playing something other than basketball. However, reality returned and we focused on the task at hand.

We were decked out in red and white velveteen uniforms that fit and had white warm-ups with red trim. They were, to coin a phrase, seeking their destiny and the ball was in their court. Prayer was still in vogue and team captain Frank Edgar from Hampton, Virginia asked God to bless both teams and keep everyone safe. After all, it was a Presbyterian Church School. I added a little prayer of my own asking God to help me not to drop the ball. It wasn't the Southeastern Conference, but it was college and no one could have been prouder. There may be unreachable stars, but if one reaches for them who knows how far they can go.

There is always a moment to remember when one realizes that a dream has come true. My moment came in the junior year when King was playing Emory and Henry College. Emory was four times larger than King and they did give some scholarships. We were located twenty miles from Emory and were arch rivals.

King had not beaten Emory in the years that we had competed. It was, to say the least, a charged up team along with the whole student body and faculty. Preparation the week before the game was intense and focused on the objective: beat Emory and Henry. It was an exciting time to be part of a dream that had dared to let me travel back in years to the makeshift arena where I always won. This was not make-believe. It was the real thing and I was a part of it.

Finally, Saturday came and there was a hush that enveloped the campus. Team members arrived early in the afternoon and went to the mess hall for the pre-game meal. Team members then went to the gym for a nap or a quiet rest before getting dressed for the game. No talking was allowed and each player was concentrating on the game. Rest time soon ended, ankles were wrapped, and all was ready.

Pre-game warm up provided opportunities to study the strengths of the Emory team. Warm ups were over as the teams retreated to the dressing room for last minute instructions. The time had arrived as the players came back to midcourt for the tipoff. The game was underway and the teams were evenly matched; the game was nip and tuck with the lead changing hands several times. The game was into the last minute and Emory was leading by six points. It didn't look good for the home team. My roommate Dillard "Zeke" Keen and I had played one of the best games of our careers. The last minute was frantic with Zeke and me leading the way.

The ball went to me at midcourt and I took two dribbles and shot. The ball swished through the net for two points. It would have been a three pointer, but there was no three point baskets at that time. The ball changed hands again and I hit another similar shot since no one came out that far to guard me. Emory hit the next shot and King was down two points. Again, the ball went to the top of the key, but this time I was guarded closely. I saw Zeke coming across the middle and passed the ball to him. His shot hit nothing but net making the deficit two points. King got the ball with fifteen seconds and it came to me. I was outside the arc and was not guarded closely. I was thinking that I could not hit another bomb with only ten seconds left, but I did. The score was tied and I turned around as if I was going back down the court but I turned quickly to intercept the inbound pass. Alas, this is not one of those happy endings story, because the referee called a foul on me. Of course I didn't touch him. The first foul shot was wide of the mark, but the second one found the bottom of the net, and Emory beat us by one point. It was a near miss and the closest King came to beating Emory during the four years I was in school.

King College Tornado Basketball Team

The Unlikely Journey to play basketball culminated in the
fulfillment of a dream. My quest was reached when I donned the
red and white velvet uniform of the King
College basketball team: The unreachable star
was reachable after all.

The dream that Mother and I cherished was to see me graduate from high school and go to college. The term, "going" to college involved more than just getting into college. It meant earning a degree and becoming successful in the world. She did not know all the implications, but she did know that a college degree and success in the business and professional world were inseparable.

The stage was set and the quest was mine to pursue. Success in high school was not an indication of success in college. Previous successes are an indication of possible success, but no guarantee unless there was a considerable amount of effort forthcoming. Mastery of course content was only part of becoming an educated person. Knowledge of basic subject matter was essential, but the utilization of that course content to solve problems is also essential. Loosely translated, that means a lot of hard work is required to receive a college degree. There were times when I thought about dropping out and joining the army or air force. The fear of failure and giving up on the dream soon brought me back to sanity and helped me to focus on the task at hand.

The top of the academic record was not endangered by my accomplishments, but I managed to keep a respectable grade point average. The only course that eluded me was calculus. An illness resulted in the loss of several classes and upon return to class the professor informed me that there would be no more scheduled classes. Each student was to take the textbook and master it at their own pace and if any one got stuck they should schedule a meeting to see him. It was completely foreign to me and after two or three weeks of frustration, I simply stopped worrying about the class. Mid semester reports indicated a grade of "Withdrew Failing" and I was unaware of the effect that the grade WF had on the grade point average.

It wasn't long after midterms began that I received a note in the mailbox from an unexpected source. It was a note from the President of the college! Dr. R. T. L. Liston wanted to see me in his office at the earliest convenience. What could I have done to warrant this request? No time was wasted in scheduling a conference with Dr. Liston. The scheduled conference time arrived and I was a puzzled student; apprehensive to say the least, as I approached the very official looking office of the President. His personal secretary was very friendly as she escorted me into his office. Pleasantries were exchanged and we talked about the part of Virginia where I grew up. The President knew more about the area than I did, and he also knew more about me than I expected.

We must have been talking for at least a half hour when the president informed me that he had not heard me say what he wanted to hear. Puzzled, I asked respectfully what that was. He responded in a friendly but stern voice and said, "I have not heard an indication that you want to continue your college education." A light came on and began to shine. I realized that Dr. Liston knew that I had not registered for classes for the next semester. I indicated that I wanted to go to school more than anything in the world, but had simply run out of money.

In a kind and friendly voice he instructed me to stop by the Registrar's office on the way out and register for next semester classes. He also instructed me to check with the Treasurer who had a note to sign for expenses. I was to follow this procedure for the remainder of my college career at King. The loan was unsecured with a three percent interest rate that would not become effective until graduation. I was stunned and managed to say thank you as I got up to leave. It was obvious that he was not finished when he said, "There is another small matter that needs our attention." It was a matter that I wanted to forget, but the issue of the WF grade on the record would not go away and Dr. Liston knew about it. I explained what had happened and that the professor had decided to have everyone work at their own pace and no one would attend class. After a few unsuccessful attempts to unlock the mysteries of calculus, I had ceased to give the matter further consideration.

I was told in no uncertain terms that issues like this could not be left dangling. Upon learning that no test had been administered and there was no opportunity to evaluate class participation, the designated grade would be changed from WF to WP. Grade point average would not be affected as much as it could have been. I didn't know it, but I could have been in deep trouble had someone not been looking out for me. But the President of the College?

One condition of the loan was that I had to work in the summers to pay what I could afford toward the account. I was able to earn enough to pay for books and supplies and continued to sign notes for room, board and tuition. Upon graduation, I owed more than four thousand dollars which was eventually repaid. My wife Phyllis shared that debt with me for two years after we were married. King sent periodic statements of the account status, but we were never pressured to settle the debt. A five hundred dollar scholarship and the support and guidance from a most unusual man were the catalysts that propelled a poor unsophisticated youngster from the region called "Appalachia," to heights that neither he nor his mother could have envisioned.

King College subsidized the AB degree for Jim Stiltner. I had a scholarship of $500 dollars from the Rotary Club in

Grundy, an academic scholarship from King and a work scholarship from King. The remainder of the cost was underwritten by personal loans from the college. Each semester notes were signed for the amount that could not be paid. Three percent interest was added, but did not become effective until after graduation. It took four years to repay the notes, but they were paid in full as agreed. Part of the agreement for the loans was that earnings from summer work would be applied to the debt that was owed to the college. What little was earned usually was quickly used up to buy textbooks the following school year.

University of Virginia Rotunda

King College Chapel

KEEP IT IN THE MIDDLE OF
THE ROAD

The following vignette is an account of the extent to which I went to fulfill my part of the gentleman's agreement. The information contained herein is not recommended for inclusion in a "How-to Manual" and it certainly should not be tried at home. The setting is the summer following the freshman year at King. I was in desperate need of a job to earn money to pay some of the expenses that would be waiting when school began. The job market in Grundy was not brimming with possibilities and a foray into the white collar industry turned up nothing. It was also not much better in the blue collar sector. However, when there was a need, it seemed that someone was there to give a helping hand. Help in this instance came from an unexpected source. I went to Sunday school and church when I was in Grundy. Mr. Robert Gibson was the teacher of the class for young adults and I attended the class.

Mr. Gibson was new to me since I had been away at school. As the members of the class gathered, they became acquainted and talked about general matters. Bob was interested in what the first year at King had been like. We talked about experiences and I mentioned that I was looking for a summer job to help cover expenses for next year. It was time for the class to begin and the conversation ended. The lesson concluded and we got up to leave, but before I reached the door Bob asked me to stay for a minute. He didn't take much time to get to the point, which was a characteristic I would observe more than a few times over the summer. He asked, "Can you drive? And do you have a driver's license?" The answer to both questions was yes. His response was, "You have a job. Report to the plant in the morning at seven a.m."

I could hardly believe what had just transpired, but did manage to say thank you and indicate I would be at the plant bright and early the next morning. We left to go our separate ways and I needed to find the "plant." It turned out the plant was the Levisa Oil Corporation which was the area distributor of Gulf Oil products and DuPont explosives. I found the plant, which consisted of a small office, a large warehouse, three very large holding tanks, and an open area that had stacks and stacks of large drums of oil and grease. I soon learned that each drum of oil or grease weighed 550 pounds. Those numbers were significant because I would be unloading, loading and stacking those drums.

I wondered how much help a 125 pound weakling would be able to provide in loading the drums of oil, but we are getting ahead of the story. Sleep that Sunday night was fitful at best, and I dreamed erratically as I slipped in and out of sleep.

Morning came and true to my word, I caught a ride and was at the plant at seven. James Chaffee, the office manager, met me at the door and gave me an invoice and delivery instructions for a load of gasoline. He informed me that the tanker was loaded and ready to go. I turned and saw the big, orange tanker truck waiting to test out its new "greenhorn" driver. It is difficult to imagine what my facial expression was as I turned and slowly approached the gasoline truck. The predawn conditions probably served as a cover for at least a dozen different emotions that I was experiencing. A debate was going on inside my head and I wasn't certain which side was winning. Should I just tell them that I had NEVER driven a truck much less a gasoline tanker truck? It was not a semi-trailer truck, but it did have the capacity to deliver 1,500 gallons of gasoline. The debate was won or lost on the strength of the argument that it was essential to have a summer job.

I approached the truck and proceeded to kick each tire to check for possible problems. I had seen other truckers on the road conduct the same test so it must be important. At any rate, it bought some more time. I climbed in the "cockpit"– at least that is what it looked like – and began to familiarize myself with the dials, gauges and gears. How difficult could this be? After all, I had obtained a driver's permit at least a year ago. Well, for starters, the car in which I had learned to drive had three forward gears, and this truck had *eight* forward gears. I located the starter and the engine roared to life; the "die" was cast. A silent prayer was uttered asking God to help find one of those gears to take me out of the plant and across the railroad tracks. Once across the railroad tracks, I would be out of sight of the plant and have a quarter mile of unpaved road before reaching the highway to learn how to drive this orange monster. Finally, I found a gear that moved the truck forward, and I was on the way.

The unpaved road proved to be a lifesaver as there was time to engage in serious trial and error with the gears. Did I fail to mention that one of my dreams Sunday night was about how to drive a truck? Cross my heart and hope to die if it is not the truth. The only problem was that the gears were much easier to manipulate in the dream than in reality.

It took several attempts to find the appropriate gears to drive on the highway. I just had to remember to double clutch to change from one gear to another. So long as the other traffic stayed out of the way and the truck could stay in one of the higher gears, everything went smoothly. It was the gearing up and down that complicated matters. The load of gasoline was to be delivered to the Races Fork coal dock near Hurley, Virginia, which meant there was a mountain between us and the destination. Well, so much for driving all the way in high gear.

Changing gears had been a battle all the way to the destination, but the dreaded sound of metal against metal had improved as the trip proceeded. A little confidence began to return and the ride became rather pleasant. The drop-off point should be a nice level area where the gasoline could easily be delivered. I expected the trip back to the plant to be smoother. Was that assumption ever wide of the mark!

The place was a beehive of activity. There were eighteen or twenty trucks laden with coal waiting to deposit their contents into railroad cars that would transport it to markets far and wide. The coal trucks were lined up to take their turn to unload and return to the mines for another load. The coal truck drivers visited or made small talk until it was their turn to unload. No time was wasted in the process and one had better be ready when their turn came.

Forget the wishful thinking that there would be a nice, level area to unload the gasoline. Access to the in-ground tank was the same route taken by the coal trucks. I had to leave the highway, drive down a dirt incline, cross a low-water bridge and up another dirt incline on the other side to reach the loading area. The bright, orange gasoline truck was easily distinguished and, with its cargo, was allowed to move in front of the next coal truck to be unloaded.

The move from the highway to the incline down to the low-water bridge was easy enough because it was all downhill. Several attempts to cross the low-water bridge and go up the other side were met with no success.

Frustration and embarrassment overwhelmed me as each attempt to climb the hill ended by "killing" the engine. Finally, the driver of the truck next in line came over and opened the truck door and told me to push the clutch to the floor. He took the gearshift, shoved it into gear and said, "Try that one." The truck moved up the hill without a hitch, and I was relieved, but if there had been a hole large enough, I would have crawled into it.

The trip back to the plant was uneventful in light of the painful lesson just experienced. Jim Chaffee asked how the trip went and the response was, "It was a piece of cake!"

PART THREE | *Occupations*

Jim Delivering Explosive Powder 1955

A SUMMER JOB

A summer job was not only a means to earn some money to help with expenses for college; it was also not without its opportunities for growth and development. I was indeed fortunate to secure a job that allowed me to make some money and to experience the world of work. The salary of seventy-five cents per hour with time and a half for overtime was very generous, but did not include "flight pay" for some of the dangerous situations and conditions that I would encounter. There was never a dull moment for a novice in the oil distribution business. The Levisa Gulf Oil Corporation was also the distribution headquarters for

E.I. DuPont explosives. The explosives were sold to the small coal mines in the area.

The veteran employees took great delight in observing how long it would take the "hot shot" college boy to learn the ropes at the plant. Everything was new to me and I was eager to learn. There was a ritual for all new employees and the nature of the work was such that it invited a bit of harassing. For instance, there were certain techniques which simplified the unloading, moving, and stacking of the oil products. Getting the 550 pound drums of grease from the railroad boxcar to the ground and to the stacking area located fifty yards away was no simple task.

As it turned out, I had to learn how to load them onto the trucks and to stack the drums of oil and grease four drums high by myself on several occasions. No. There were no modern devices like forklifts to provide assistance. I would have help some of the time but not until the other workers had a hearty laugh at my futile attempts to tip over one of the grease-laden drums. There is a technique to it.

Grease and oil were delivered by rail, usually one boxcar every two weeks, and it took one day to unload it. There were no forklifts or other mechanical devices to aid in unloading the cargo of oil products. I simply had to tip over a drum of grease, roll it to three wooden boards that formed an incline from the boxcar and the ground, and let it roll down the incline to a sand pit. The drums of grease were then rolled by hand to the storage area and stacked four barrels high. The first boxcar of oil and grease arrived shortly after I started working. The grizzled veterans were ready and waiting for the rookie to show. Some of them delayed their gasoline deliveries to help me get started with the unloading. I saw no mechanical means by which the contents of the boxcar could be unloaded so I asked how the oil and grease got from the railroad car to the storage area. It was simple they said. Just jump up in the car, turn the drum of grease over and let it roll down the incline.

No one moved so I assumed it was my responsibility to unload the first drum. I jumped up into the boxcar and grabbed the first drum and proceeded to tip it over on its side. Whoa! Have you ever tried to tip over a 550 pound of anything, let alone a drum of grease? No amount of pulling, pushing, grunting, lifting, and cursing would move the barrel. I was instructed that a good pair of gloves might help to get the job done. I donned the gloves, but the result was the same...the drum had not moved. After several suggestions, which they knew would not work, and after they had enjoyed themselves at my expense, I was shown the technique that helped to overturn the drum of grease. The trick was to add weight to the weight of the drum of grease and start a rocking motion until the weight tipped it over. One thing remaining was to make certain that it didn't fall on my toes. The need to wear steel toed shoes was clearly evident. The initiation was complete; the only thing left was to empty the car of its cargo.

Accompanying the drums of grease and oil were 2,500 to 3,000 cases of oil that had to be unloaded. Once I learned how to unload and stack the drums of oil and grease, my work was defined for two days. Unloading and stacking the cases of oil was a different animal. It took two people to remove the cases of oil from rollers that extended from the boxcar to the warehouse, and stack them eight cases high. Usually, one person placed the oil on the rollers and two workers took them off and stacked them. The last two cases had to be lifted over our heads. A day spent unloading and stacking a carload of oil was a sure cure for insomnia.

The DuPont explosives were treated in a similar manner. Instead of being shipped in by rail, they were delivered by tractor trailer trucks. The explosives were delivered by a driver and one helper. They arrived at night and were ready to unload by the crack of dawn. The dynamite was stored in what was called magazines located several hundred yards away from anything. A series of rollers similar to those used to unload the cases of oil extended from the truck to the magazine. The delivery of the powder and caps was made by truckers who wasted no time in unloading their cargo. The boxes of explosives had to be stacked, as in the cases of oil, eight high with the last two hoisted above one's head. It was like pumping iron for two hours. I had help because it took two people to keep up with the two truckers who were in a hurry to unload and be on their way. I received the first wooden box of dynamite and timidly started the stack. My helper, who was from the plant, informed me that the boxes would come off the rollers in a hurry. I knew what he meant when I turned to receive the next box. Three of the boxes had fallen off the rollers while I was handling a single case. The helper from the plant demonstrated the technique. He grabbed the next case, slammed it to the floor and turned to get another box. I expected to be blown away any minute. *Oh well, you only live once,* I thought.

The trailer was unloaded and the drivers of the truck quickly moved to their next assignment. Tired as I was, I loaded twenty cases of explosives, dropped the helper off at the plant, and proceeded to deliver the dynamite to a "drift mouth" mining location on Poplar Creek. Jim Chaffee had told me that the mines on Poplar Creek were in need of the powder since they had emptied their magazine that morning. The site was three fourths of a mile up the side of the mountain and the dirt road was not as much of a road as it was a path.

There are two types of coal mines, the drift mouth and the shaft mines. The drift mouth mine is one in which a seam of coal is located and the coal is extracted by digging back into the side of the mountain. The shaft mine is one which relinquishes its fossil fuel to efforts that penetrate downward toward the center of the earth. Once a seam of coal is located, the layer of coal is removed from between the layers of rock. The shaft may be anywhere from one hundred yards to a half mile or more below the surface. Depending upon the height of the seam of coal, it is removed by hand or machinery. The height of the layer of coal that can be mined ranges from eight to ten feet and as low as thirty-six inches. Both operations utilize explosives to loosen the coal which is then transported to the surface and sent to markets all over the world.

Another method of coal mining is called "strip mining." If the coal is near enough to the surface, it can be mined by bulldozing the top of the terrain down to the coal and scooping the black gold up and hauling it away in heavy-duty trucks.

It staggers the mind to realize that men are willing to travel for a mile or more back into the mountain to load coal by shovel in a space that is no higher than thirty-six to forty inches. The luxury of working in coal seams that were considerably higher, like five to eight feet, belonged to the large coal companies. The smaller mines were left with the unenviable alternative of extracting the coal where the use of mechanized devices was severely limited. At best, coal mining for the men who go into the bowels of the earth to make a living is an extremely dangerous profession. Notwithstanding the claustrophobic nature of the job, the very thought of extracting a layer of the earth that is supporting the earth above gives testimony to the precarious nature of the work.

Placing timbers where the coal is removed provides some support, but how much can the earth be disturbed before the top comes crashing down? My father was a coal miner and he came home more than once with angry scrapes down his side where tons of rock had fallen close enough to cause him to say, "I came close to meeting my Master today."

My help for unloading the dynamite on this particular day was the driver who operated the semi-tractor to deliver gasoline. He had to deliver a load of gasoline to Jewel Smokeless Coal Company near Richlands, Virginia and could not help with the delivery of the explosives to Poplar Creek. He knew what a difficult job it was to deliver the explosives to the mine on Poplar Creek Mountain and I suspected the driver had arranged to have someone at Jewel Smokeless call in an order for gasoline.

Truth is they didn't need the gasoline, but it gave "Red" an excuse for getting out of the delivery of the explosives. However, he did take time to offer a few suggestions. His warning about a copperhead snake that had been seen near the path to the magazine did nothing to quiet uneasiness about this trip. He also indicated that the boxes of caps used to trigger the dynamite should be carried in the cab of the truck instead of in the back with the cases of black powder. His caution to be careful with the caps served only to raise the blood pressure. With that, he threw two boxes of caps to me and watched as I juggled and finally held on to the highly sensitive triggers for the dynamite. With those words of wisdom he left the delivery of the dynamite to the college boy.

I was extremely cautious on The Poplar Creek run. It was a treacherous trip even in the best of times, and an early morning rain didn't help matters. Extreme caution was the password for the day, since the destination was nearly at the top of the mountain. The road was narrow and winding with several switchbacks to make it even more precarious. The old ticker was pounding furiously and my blood pressure must have been off the charts. The truck was in the lowest gear and I inched slowly up the side of the mountain until I was within five hundred yards of the destination. I was on the path leading to the powder magazine. The path itself was another fifty yards and that meant twenty trips carrying one box each trip! How long would that take, I wondered.

Suddenly, the road narrowed even more and appeared to be partially washed away. I stopped the truck and got out to take a closer look. It had rained earlier in the day and a part of the dirt road was indeed gone. One might say I was on the horns of a dilemma.

There was not room to turn around, no way to go forward, no possibility of backing off the mountain, and I certainly was not going to tote twenty boxes, each weighing forty pounds, up the mountain for 550 yards. That was roughly the length of six football fields laid end to end!

The cell phone had not yet been invented and it was quite possible that there was not a house within a five mile radius from which a call could be made to the plant. Decisions, decisions. Something had to be done even if it was wrong. No. That's the wrong statement. This had to be the right decision or I might blow the side of the mountain away, me included. It was not a snap decision, but a walk down the mountain seemed to be the best alternative. Once off the mountain, there was a need to find a telephone. To the delight of the novice gasoline truck driver turned high explosives truck driver, a house was nearby with a telephone. The residents were happy to let me use their phone to call the plant. The situation was explained to Jim Chaffee and much to my surprise, found that he was the only one at the plant and the miners were in serious need of the dynamite. You are the driver and it is your responsibility to deliver the powder as promised was his advice. I was on my own with a truck loaded with explosives perched on the side of the mountain that could start sliding any minute. I had not received the response that I expected. In fact, I had envisioned a response something like, "Just stay where you are and we will send some help." It wasn't at all what I wanted to hear, especially since a pretty young lady lived in the house where I sought help and we had struck up a conversation. The excuse I had for staying longer was squashed, and I was forced to attend to business.

The trek back up the mountain found the truck as I had left it. After thinking the problem through, I decided to try to shore up the washed out portion of the road. No tools were available, so I rolled the largest rocks that could be moved into the washed away part of the road. It didn't appear to be very stable, but it would have to do.

I opened the door and slid under the steering wheel with some trepidation and started the engine. The truck roared to life and moved slowly to the newly "repaired" break in the road. If it didn't hold, the truck and its contents, including me, would slide off the road and tumble down the mountainside until the dynamite exploded. The front wheels rolled over the patched up road and it held; my breathing became a bit easier. However, as the hind wheels moved across the breach, the truck started to slide. I hastily started to consider the options, one of which was to leap out of the truck. It was fortunate that I did not act on that option, because the truck stopped its slide into oblivion and rolled past the trouble spot and moved without further incident to the path leading to the magazine. Just how close I was to oblivion, will never be known. There had been enough excitement for one day as the first box of explosives was lifted to my shoulders with only nineteen cases to go. The path was overgrown with weeds up to my waist and I suddenly remembered the caution about the copperhead. It was going to be a long afternoon. I moved tentatively along the path thinking that each step might result in a snake bite. I had not gone more than a third of the way to the magazine before I quickly stopped in mid stride and backed away. Had I taken the next step, it would have been right beside the coiled copperhead that was enjoying the sun from a rock located on the side of the path. I slowly backed away and looked for something that could be used to at least put a scare into the snake.

The only thing I found was a piece of a two by four that had been sawed off to make a triangle with three sharp sides. I picked it up and with a flick of the wrist launched it like a knife thrower would throw toward a target. At best, I hoped to scare the snake away, but it did not move. As I hurriedly searched for another rock or anything to throw, it became apparent why the snake had not scurried away. The sharp edge of the wooden block had struck the neck of the snake just behind its head and severed it completely with the exception of a thin strip of skin. Who was guiding my hand this day? Then I remembered the saying, "where you find one copperhead snake there would be another one nearby." Relief came only when the last box of black powder was placed in the magazine.

The explosives were unloaded, the door to the magazine was locked securely and the trek back down the mountain began. It occurred to me the men at the plant would not believe my story about the snake, so I gathered it up and dumped it in the back of the truck as proof positive the dragon had been slain. The descent down the mountain was completed in careful mode, especially the area where the road had been "repaired." Less pressure was exerted on the repairs on the way down, so the ride was much easier with much less tension.

The trip back to the plant was like a drive in the park, and I suddenly realized I was very tired. I had the feeling that it was going to be an interesting summer. I rolled into the plant and was met by Jim the office manager. He wanted to know how the day had gone. "It was a piece of cake," I responded, whereupon he said, "I knew you could do it." Jim sought out "Red," the semi-truck driver and informed him that there was a present in the back of the truck for him and then went about the remainder of the day's activities. It had been a hectic day and I again had gained some confidence as I was faced with a number of obstacles which I had been fortunate enough to overcome. I grew some that summer and it was another example of having an attitude of I *can* do it, rather than I *can't* do it.

The summer held several interesting incidents such as the one just described. One episode involved the delivery of gasoline to a truck dealership. The path to the tank where the gasoline was to be delivered was very narrow and I needed to have someone direct me as I backed to the drop site. I asked a youngster, who was standing nearby if he would watch as I backed the truck down the narrow road. He agreed. Everything was going smoothly, but I felt the need to be sure he was not getting too close to a huge drop off. It was a good thing I stopped to look. Had the rear truck tires turned one more full rotation, he, the truck, and the load of gasoline would have ended up at the bottom of the ravine. A little distraught I asked why he had not indicated how close the truck was to falling into the ravine. His response was, "You didn't tell me to say stop. You just said to watch." Never trust anyone to direct the process of backing a vehicle.

INTO THE WILD BLUE YONDER: DECISION TIME

T here are a number of times in life that decisions are made which beg the question: "what if?" What would have been the consequences and implications if the alternative choice had been selected? A defining moment in my life was instrumental in determining the type of person I would become and how it would affect thousands of people. It was one of those crossroads that presented an opportunity to make a decision of life changing proportions. The situation came about quite unexpectedly and by accident. Two Navy recruiters were on campus to talk with students who might be interested in a career in the U.S. Navy. They were interested in seniors, who were scheduled to graduate in May, 1957.

Gerald Enos, the senior class president, was in a hurry to get across campus. As he came near, he approached and asked what I was doing for the next half hour. "Not anything important," I responded. Jerry indicated that he needed an audience. I was not interested in joining the Navy, but at Jerry's insistence I agreed to listen to what they had to say.

We arrived at the Hay Building and joined ten or fifteen people who had gathered to hear the presentation. At the conclusion of the general presentation everyone left with the exception of Jerry, John Sadler, Robert Sanford and me.

I had no idea why I stayed, but was fascinated at the possibility of a career in the Navy. The specific program for which they were recruiting was the Aviation Officers Cadet training to develop jet pilots for the Navy. It suddenly became more fascinating than ever. At the conclusion of the training, those who were successful would become commissioned officers. The idea of being a jet pilot for the U.S. Navy was a once in a lifetime experience.

The Navy recruiters were ready to proceed to the next step, but more information was needed before the young men could make a commitment. The recruiters indicated that acceptance into the program was contingent upon meeting requirements. They left application forms with the four of us with instructions to complete and submit them if we were interested in entering the program. The Navy would provide air transportation to Atlanta, Georgia, where a series of tests and examinations would be administered to determine whether or not anyone qualified for the program. The mental, physical, and psychological tests were to be administered, along with time in simulation activities. Lectures would fill the gap on any data not covered in the testing.

Navy brass wanted to assure themselves that individuals selected for training were worth the time and money, and the four young men were interested in knowing enough to make an informed decision about this new and exciting program. The meeting concluded and Jerry, Bob, John, and I had a wrap session about the program and what our next step should be. The four of us agreed to accept the invitation to go to Atlanta and pursue the possibility of a career in the Navy. Applications were completed and mailed. No time was wasted and four round-trip tickets were received days later. If memory serves well, the three nights in Atlanta were Friday, Saturday, and Sunday with a return flight to Tri Cities Airport in Johnson City, Tennessee, on Monday so that there was a minimum of class time lost.

The day of departure was not a good introduction to the "friendly skies." In fact, the skies were not friendly at all. It was my first flight and would prove to be an experience that I would not soon forget. The four would-be-pilots arrived at the airport ready to start their trip to Atlanta with the weather looking ominous and subject to getting worse. We arrived at the airport wondering whether or not the planes were flying. The ceiling was almost at ground level and to make matters worse, the fog had rolled in quickly.

There were mixed feelings about flying in weather that was so bad it had the airport officials concerned. However, the arrival of the incoming flight was announced as we peered into the fog and clouds. We could hear the roar of the engines, but were unable to see the plane until it dropped out of the clouds and onto the runway. The question remained as to whether or not the plane would continue the flight to Atlanta. I, personally, preferred to have the flight crew be able to see where they were going. Of course, the plane was equipped with instruments that helped the pilot to "see." After a delay, the flight was called and we boarded and found our seats. The weather still was not good, but the decision was made to continue the flight. I was seated next to a very pregnant young lady. She had been on the incoming flight and had become ill because of the rough weather. As the plane ascended into the murky sky, the stewardess, as they were called, informed us that it might be a bumpy ride and we should keep our seat belts securely fastened. She also pointed to some air sickness bags located at each seat back that could be used in case someone became sick.

Unfortunately, the inevitable happened and the young mother-to-be filled one bag and needed more. I turned in the seat so I could not see her because I was on the verge of needing one myself. I knew that if I looked at her I would lose what I had eaten for breakfast that morning. I was very sorry to be so unsociable, but had to fight nausea all the way to Atlanta. I wondered what the Navy would say if I informed them that I became ill on the flight from Tri Cities. I decided not tell them. Safely on the ground at our destination, we were met by the Navy brass and recruiters their guests for the next three and a half days. The four of us were joined by six other young men who were there for the same reason. The testing began and every minute of the time on the base was filled with the most rigorous examinations anyone could imagine. The only time we were not being tested was when we were eating or sleeping.

Results of the testing were shared with all participants and four of us passed the tests and met all the qualifications: Bob, Jerry, John and I. The four from King. We had come to the proverbial crossroads and a decision was forthcoming that would define, to an extent, the type of people we would become.

The Navy extended an invitation and we were faced with a decision about which path to choose. There was a kicker which the four did not know about until the results were determined. If we did not accept the invitation, our records would be sent to our respective draft boards and we would be placed at the top of the list to be drafted into the army, which meant we were subject to be drafted at any time.

The Navy wanted to assure themselves that the individuals chosen would be worth their time and effort. They had to protect their investment and make certain that trainees could be trusted with a million dollar airplane. They also wanted to make certain that individuals selected would be going into the program with their eyes open. At that time, statistics showed that one out of every three planes crashed.

Their description of landing on an aircraft carrier was interesting. It was described as something akin to trying to land on a dime that was bobbing up and down in the ocean while moving forward. Something to think about. The King College Four as we came to be known on campus had been presented with a challenge that would surely change the direction of our lives. Ultimately, we would choose one path. To fly, or not to fly, that is the question. We returned to campus to ponder the decision.

Ironically, only one of the four chose to enter the AOC program and became a jet pilot for the Navy. John Sadler chose to accept the Navy's call to duty. He retired from the Navy and became a preacher. Jerry decided to teach for a time and then chose to join the Marine Corps. He did not become a pilot due to health reasons. Bob worked in several areas, principally in the textile industry. He was kidded when asked about the line of clothing in which he specialized. His answer was, "I am in ladies underwear." So what else is new? It was a struggle for me, but I decided to pass on the opportunity and become an educator. It was a tough decision and I often wondered what life would have been like as a Navy jet pilot.

The Navy was true to their word. They sent records to the local draft board and my name was placed at the top of the list to be called to active duty in the army. It stayed there for the next eight years. There were no wars, engagements, or skirmishes that called for additional draftees during that time and I was not drafted. In fact, the matter was forgotten until I had occasion to visit my hometown and was contacted by the local draft board. The Director of the draft board for the Buchanan County area heard that I was in town visiting relatives and called to inform us that I was on top of the list to be drafted. She asked if anything had changed. My status had changed; I was now married with a baby on the way, which was enough to move me down the list of possible draftees.

"Do you realize that we were ready to send a call for you to be drafted into the army?" To say I was surprised is an understatement. I was never called to serve. What if…? What if I had chosen to be an officer in the Navy? What if my draft board director had not chosen to call me about my classification? Is it possible, just possible, that someone was looking out for me? I think so. Otherwise I might still be trying to land a jet plane on a dime in the middle of the ocean.

Patricia and Jim on his '57 Chevy

SERENDIPITY: FINDING VALUE WITHOUT SEEKING

The day before I graduated was an absolutely perfect time to be alive. The campus was almost deserted with the exception of a few employees and staff members and a dozen or two students. Spring on the King College campus was always like a picture post card, but it had exceeded all expectations on this day. The dogwoods were just past their peak, but the campus was still clothed in the white, pink, and green that only Mother Nature could blend so perfectly. The sun shone brightly and greeted me from a great night's sleep. I had slept late and didn't feel guilty about it for the first time in what seemed to be forever. I didn't even mind missing breakfast as I ventured out to meet the rest of the day.

The squirrels scampered about and the birds appeared to sing with more gusto than usual. Could it be that they knew I was about to graduate and become an alumnus of King College? Could it have been that Mother was smiling from heaven and just would not allow anything to spoil this wonderful occasion? I felt a tinge of sadness as I remembered she was not there to celebrate the realization of our dream.

Mother would have admonished me by reminding me that she had been with me all along. I took solace in the fact that Dad, my sister Pat and my girlfriend were coming tomorrow to see the graduation ceremonies that would be the final indication that the unreachable star had been reached after all. Nothing, it appeared, could mar this day. I had that feeling of satisfaction and knowing that the race had been finished; the dream that had been shared was now a reality because we had reached out to touch a star.

Last night's speaker had said the appropriate things one expects at graduations, one of which was that they had scaled the mountain and achieved the goal. I was too busy basking in the praise of accomplishment that the significance of what the speaker had said next completely eluded me. As I remembered what the speaker said, I was jolted out of my euphoric mood and literally stopped in my tracks. The speaker had said that commencement was not an end in itself, but a beginning. It suddenly occurred to me that I was about to graduate from college and had not the faintest idea of what I was going to do.

A goal had been reached, but how did that translate to action in the cold cruel world that waited? As Dad would have said, "Does that degree guarantee you a job?" It did not. I was to be awarded a Bachelor of Arts degree in Interdepartmental Science signifying that I had mastered enough of the content in the subjects taken in the areas of science such as Chemistry, Physics, Biology, and Astronomy to earn the degree. How would this hard-earned knowledge be used to make a living?

Did someone mention that for every mountain top there was a valley? The stroll across campus became more reflective as I pondered my future. Tomorrow would be the first day of the rest of my life. I had heard that saying and it seemed to fit. Four years had been spent to obtain a liberal arts degree, but I did not know how it would affect the rest of my life.

I was concentrating on the issue to the extent that I did not realize that someone was attempting to get my attention. President Liston was calling from across campus. I could not imagine what he wanted, but I changed direction and met him near the monument to the King family who had established the college and had provided support over the years.

We shared pleasantries and spoke about the graduation activities. To my surprise he asked the question that I had been mulling over for myself. He wanted to know what my plans were for the future. I stumbled and stammered around trying to sound like I had given a lot of thought to the question and that everything was under control. Somehow Dr. Liston knew, or strongly suspected, that I was at another crossroads and the decision that begged for high priority was one that had life altering implications.

Dr. Liston suggested that I might want to talk with the Superintendent of Schools in Tazewell County, Virginia, who was on campus to recruit science teachers. I was completely surprised at the idea of actually becoming a teacher because this was the first time I truly realized that I was going to make a career of this; it became so tangible. Little did I know that this encounter would lead to such a defining moment in my life. I responded to President Liston's suggestion by indicating that I had no training as a teacher. He informed me that the first and most important requirement for being a good teacher was to have a basic knowledge of the content or subject matter to be taught. The Virginia State Department of Education had alternative procedures for issuing teaching certificates and the School Superintendent would explain them to me. Dr. Liston escorted me to the interview room and introduced me to the superintendent from Tazewell County. At the conclusion of the interview, I left with an application and an offer to teach science in Tazewell County, Virginia. What an amazing turn of events!

Everything was moving at mach speed and I was caught up in the whirlwind. Graduation day arrived and the world slowed enough to allow us to enjoy the moment they had looked forward to for the past four years. Dad and Pat were there to celebrate with me and that was special in itself. It was the first time that any of my family had the opportunity to see me participate in any events since leaving high school.

Dad had gotten a steady job and conditions at home were much improved. Pat was growing up, and Ruby was graduating from high school and was going to be a student at King College. Her journey was as challenging as was mine, but she climbed the mountains and became a success that should be recorded.

Something new had also been added at home. Dad had purchased a car and it was the first automobile he had driven since he wrecked a Model T Ford about the time I was born. He had nearly died, so owning another car had not been a high priority for him. Having access to transportation, other than hitchhiking, was a welcome change.

The necessity for transportation figured prominently in the decision regarding a career in education, or for that matter any other career choice. Except for an occasional loan of Dad's car, I was without transportation. The offer to teach in Tazewell County came with the huge salary of $2,400 per year. A decision to teach – and it appeared to be the best alternative – meant I needed to rent a place to live, be able to pay the bills, and find some way to get from one place to another, all on $2,400 per year before taxes.

It occurred to me that the Buchanan County Schools might be in need of a science teacher. Wouldn't that be a kick in the head to teach at my old high school? A trip to the courthouse and a conference with Percy V. Dennis who was superintendent revealed a need for a science teacher at Grundy High School. In fact, he matched the offer from Tazewell and added another hundred dollars per month to drive a school bus. Voile! A job with transportation to and from work and I could stay at home for free. It may not have been the path less travelled, but it was a life changing decision.

The transition from student to teacher was not an easy one. On the job training was not new, but the first two years I struggled to stay up with the students. Basic knowledge of subject matter was crucial and the teaching techniques and procedures were just as important to the learning process. I enjoyed teaching, but my aspirations were to become an administrator in education.

An administrative position was in the realm of possibility and would come in due time. The immediate task at hand was to get ready to meet my first class where I was the teacher rather than the student. It was a challenge that demanded a change in lifestyle. I was only three years older than some of the students and many of them attended the same church and frequented the same social activities. I laid down the rules and announced that I would not play favorites. Any friends or family members who happened to be in school were students and I was the teacher.

The experience at Grundy High School was invaluable. Since I was young, single, and had lots of time there were many demands on my time. I drove the school bus, taught five classes, coached basketball, was one of the senior class sponsors, drove the bus to the away games for basketball, football, and track, and coached the golf team. There was never a dull moment.

A funny thing happened on the way to the golf match. The opening of school was a time to organize for activities other than academic teaching assignments. Money was not plentiful so many of the teachers volunteered for extracurricular activities including some of the minor sports teams. It was a labor of love because there was no pay for what they did. There was no lack of opportunity to be involved and I was no exception. I had my quota, which was considerable, since I was single with plenty of free time to spare.

Well into the school year, a group of young men approached me with an unusual request. Spokesman for the group was an extraordinarily gifted athlete who played all sports equally well. His right arm was in a cast and sling because it had been broken in an accident. The young man, whose name was Gary Thompson, indicated that they wanted me to be the coach for the golf team they hoped to organize. My response was, "Surely you must be kidding, I've never played golf in my life." They responded by saying I didn't need to coach them, instead a faculty member was required to develop a schedule, set play dates to compete with other schools, and supervise them when they practiced and were assembled as a team. I was still skeptical and indicated it was something that I knew nothing about. Gary stopped any further protest when he laid down the challenge. He said, "If I play with one arm, will you be our coach?" How could I say no to that? Obviously, the team was organized and Grundy High School had its first golf team and a novice coach.

The season was a success for the team. Not only did Gary play with one arm, he was the top player on the golf ladder. He won most of his matches and led the team to the

Virginia State finals held in Chantilly which is now the Dulles International Airport. The team did not win the state title, but represented their school very well.

One fly in the ointment was a tradition observed by the coaches of competing teams. They played behind the players and it was an insult to refuse to participate. All the coaches were golfers, and then there was me. It was easily the most embarrassing situation I had encountered. I found out about the tradition of the coaches playing behind the teams at the first match of the season, and with borrowed clubs I teed the ball up and proceeded to score twenty-five or thirty on the first two holes and then my game fell apart. The embarrassment forced me to seek help. Gary tutored me all season and by the time it was over the golf bug had bitten and I became a fairly good golfer.

My teaching experience included three years at Grundy High School and two years at Huguenot High School in Chesterfield County. On the job training was not new, but the first two years found me struggling to stay up with the students. Basic knowledge of subject matter was crucial, but the teaching techniques and procedures were just as important to the learning process. I enjoyed teaching, but my aspirations were to become an administrator in education. My penchant for educational administration demanded more formal education that paralleled a career in education. New horizons opened as it became possible to take a leave of absence from teaching to pursue a graduate degree in Supervision and Administration. A summer session at the University of Virginia, followed by a full session and one additional summer session earned a

Master's Degree in Educational Administration and Supervision. After the leave of absence, it was back to work not as a teacher but as an administrator.

The study skills did not have time to get rusty before the opportunity to enter another graduate program became available. However, from this point forward all formal schooling was accomplished while working full-time. Working full-time and attending classes left precious little time for the family, but it finally resulted in an Educational Specialist Degree from the prestigious College of William and Mary in Williamsburg, Virginia.

It appeared that "schooling" would never end, prompting a statement from a colleague that he would not aspire to be a life-long student like me. There was more to come. A move and change in career paths had complicated the closure for the completion of the degree from William and Mary, but Robert Maidment, a major professor, made it possible for me to complete the work for the Ed Specialist Degree in Atlanta as I settled in a new job. Additional post-graduate work was completed at Virginia Commonwealth University and the University of Virginia before plans were developed to enter the doctoral program at Georgia State University in Atlanta.

Fulfilling the requirements of being a full-time student and working full-time was possible because of the support and encouragement of wife Phyllis, sons Brian and Chris, Joseph M. Johnston, and the members of the Commission on Secondary and Middle Schools of the Southern Association of Colleges and Schools (SACS). The terminal degree of Doctor of Philosophy or Ph.D. in Educational

Leadership was conferred by Georgia State University in 1985. Hooding ceremonies were conducted by Major Professor Everette DeVaughn of the University. I earned degrees from four institutions of higher education and am indebted to all of them, but King College is the institution that gave wings to dreams that had been part of a vision from long ago.

A career in education had been launched that spanned forty-five years and provided an opportunity to work at the local, state, national, and international levels of education. It was a career that opened vistas about which I had dreamed but had never imagined experiencing. It was the rare privilege of working and directing projects which touched the lives of hundreds of thousands of adults, and millions of students.

The career began simply enough in the classroom and reached into the unlikely environs of Heads of State, Ambassadors, Government Officials, State and Local officials, as well as School Administrators and Teachers from local, state, national, and international levels. It was a career that presented opportunities which I was certain were not managed as well as they should have been to realize their maximum potential. I was reminded of the parable of the talents in Matthew chapter twenty-five where the foolish man hid the amount of money entrusted to him and didn't invest it for the master. Whatever good could have been realized from investing the talent was lost. Many opportunities were available to me and I sometimes wonder how to answer the question, "What have you done with the abundant opportunities that have been given to you?"

Serendipity is the phenomenon of finding valuable things not sought after. I was opportunistic and believed that one should be as prepared as possible to respond to the experiences that life had to offer. My destiny would be determined not only by choosing the obvious, but also by taking the path less travelled.

A SECOND CAN BE AN ETERNITY

Who has not watched a football split the goalposts from the foot of a kicker as one last second ticks off the clock? It is the difference between winning and losing the game. Or, who has not witnessed a basketball that is in bounded, caught and launched into the air as the last second expires from the game clock? Two teams and two sets of spectators appear transfixed in time as the ball floats toward the goal. The ball swishes through the net and one group of players and fans are ecstatic and the other group is greatly disappointed. But wait! The officials ruled the last second of the game had expired before the ball left the shooters hand and the fortunes of the individuals are reversed. What a difference a tenth of a second makes.

Not every event turns on a dime or has such a dramatic effect on people. Whenever it does, lives are changed and often one is left with the question, "What if?" It is a rhetorical question in some cases, because once a person is faced with a crossroads situation and the decision is made by them or for them, the clock cannot be turned back. One is prompted to say, "It is unfair. Our team led the game for fifty nine minutes and fifty nine seconds, but the final second determined the outcome." The following vignette is included because it describes how a career hung in the balance as the clock ticked off the seconds.

It was the end of the summer session in which final preparations were in progress at the University of Virginia to recognize individuals who were graduating. One of the groups to be recognized was those who had completed requirements for the Master of Education degree. Most of the recipients of the M.Ed. degree were teachers who had been part of the program sponsored and funded by the National Science Foundation to upgrade their skills and knowledge of science.

I was in the third year of teaching at Grundy High School when I first learned about the NSF grants. The first application was submitted to the University of Wisconsin, and was rejected. In retrospect, it was a blessing in disguise. Who in his right mind would elect to spend a winter in the cold, frozen North? In the interim I moved to teach another two years at Huguenot High School near Richmond, Virginia.

The second application for a Federal grant went to the University of Virginia. In the process of making an application for the grant, it was discovered that the program at Virginia was directed by Dr. Ertle Thompson. Wonder of wonders! Professor Thompson had been my Physics teacher at Grundy High. It may have been one of those coincidences that just might have been the deciding factor in the selection for the grant. I wanted to think I had made it on my ability, but hey, who looks a gift horse in the mouth?

It was a new and exciting experience since the undergraduate degree was from King College where the total number of students was 360. Virginia was a large university with an excellent academic record and was easily one of the most beautiful spots on earth. King was a liberal arts school that, despite the difference in the size of the institutions, also had a very strong academic record. It was the perfect college for me at the time and it provided an easier transition from a small college to a larger university like Virginia. What better place to hone my academic skills after an excellent basic foundation at King. One look answers the question as to why Thomas Jefferson built his Monticello on a hill overlooking his beloved University.

The duration of the program included a summer session and a full year and one more summer session. Phyllis and I were married at the end of that summer. There were many young ladies in my life, but none were of a serious nature that would cause me to give my freedom up to become a married man. That is, not until Phyllis came into my life. I had known her most of my life, but lo and behold the little girl had grown into a beautiful young lady. We didn't rush into marriage, but after four years of courtship that was sometimes rocky and fraught with lover's quarrels, we were married August 19, 1961, in our hometown of Grundy, Virginia. I remembered moving into one of the smallest apartments I had ever seen when we settled back in Richmond. It wasn't too bad because Phyllis stayed in the apartment and continued her quest for a degree in Business Education and I went back to finish my degree work at the University of Virginia. We had weekends together as I commuted back and forth from Charlottesville to Richmond.

The absentee husband had been fortunate to be selected to live on the Range, which was usually reserved for students who had distinguished themselves academically. We know, just don't ask. The Range, for those of you who do not know, are the original buildings that were located down both sides of the Lawn and blend with the Rotunda that is displayed prominently in publications as the focal point of the University. The word campus was not used, but instead it was reverently referred to as the Grounds.

It was another mountain top that my mother and I had never dreamed about, but which had become an extension of the original dream. At any rate, I knew that she must have been proud to look from heaven and witness the crowning achievement bestowed upon her son. The significance of this moment in time came just before the march down the Lawn to receive the degree.

The event that rocketed me into a different orbit began quietly enough two days before graduation ceremonies. I had applied several weeks earlier for the position of Science Supervisor for the Richmond City School System. Dr. Francis Sisson, Director of Personnel, had granted me an interview, listened intently to a review of qualifications and experience I possessed, and blithely indicated that I was too young for the position.

Richmond was a large school division with hundreds of science teachers, many of whom were old enough to be my mother, and who would resent taking suggestions from a youngster. Dr. Sisson was probably right, and his offer to teach in the system for $5,500 dollars per year was accepted. Job security was important to a newlywed and after all, the completion of my degree was rewarded with a $1,100 raise.

A visit to Program Director Thompson's office was intended to express a hearty thank you for the opportunity to participate in the NSF program that had allowed me to earn a master's degree. The visit was very pleasant and short. As I rose to leave, Dr. Thompson asked if I would be interested in talking with Dr. Frank Kizer. I didn't know Frank Kizer, and wondered why I should speak to him. It just so happened that he was the Science Supervisor for the Virginia State Department of Education, and he was on the Grounds to interview individuals who were interested in the position of Assistant Supervisor of Science for the state of Virginia.

My first inclination was uninterested, since I had just recently interviewed for a similar position with Richmond

City only to be told I was too young for the position. I turned to leave, but stopped short when Dr. Thompson indicated that it would not hurt to speak to him. Timeout! Why not? It might be interesting to hear what he had to say. The clock on the wall said it is time to go, but I released the door and sat down to wait. Someone had said that if the professor didn't show in ten minutes, the students were free to go. So, I would give him ten minutes.

The wait became ten minutes and then fifteen minutes and I did not know what held me longer. The time seemed to drag and to fill time my eyes focused on a publication entitled, *The Evaluative Criteria, 6th Edition.* It was a publication of the National Study of School Evaluation and it was used to provide schools with the proper materials to conduct a self-evaluation or self-study. The document held my attention only briefly, but later in my career I became Chairman of the Board of Directors of the organization that published the document. Time was being wasted for no good reason and patience was a virtue, but impatience ruled the moment. One second to go.

I got up to leave and at that precise moment the door to the interview room opened and Dr. Kizer and the two individuals who had been interviewed appeared. He looked at me and asked if I was interested in talking about the position. It was the moment of decision and I was ready to say no and go about other business. Five-tenths of a second to go. Time-out. Instead, I let go of the door and said yes to the question, while muttering to myself that it was a waste of good time.

I introduced myself to Dr. Kizer who was looking at his watch as he indicated he was late for another appointment and could spare about two minutes. We had not entered the interview room and he looked again at his watch and suggested that I write him a letter indicating interest in the position and to explain why I thought I would be a good candidate for the job. How many ways are there to say the last second has ticked off the clock and the last shot rimmed out? Adios, good bye, farewell, the party's over.

My head was full of things I could have said and should have said as I left the building. I was upset with someone, but didn't know who; maybe at myself for spending so much time in a futile endeavor. The more I reflected on the interlude the more upset I became and resolved then and there to compose the best letter that Dr. Kizer would ever receive from any applicant and would explain why I was the best candidate for the position of Assistant Supervisor of Science for the State of Virginia.

Considerable time and effort went into the construction of the letter of application, and it was impressive, if I do say so myself. I researched every bit of information available on the Virginia Department of Education and especially the science supervision program that was currently in place. No stone was left unturned if it had anything to do with the position. Several revisions were completed and rejected until the letter finally reflected exactly what I wanted to say. The letter and the application were mailed and forgotten since I did not expect anything but a form letter.

Two weeks had not elapsed before an official looking letter with the State Seal of Virginia on it was delivered to me. At least my efforts had been recognized by someone in the state hierarchy. As it turned out, the State Superintendent of Public Education himself was impressed with the letter of application. To shorten an already long story, I was offered the position and accepted it to be under the direct supervision of Dr. Franklin Kizer. The ball swished through the net as the last tenth of a second ticked off the clock and the home team won. My life was turned 180 degrees and it had happened in the twinkling of an eye.

IT WAS THE BEST OF TIMES

T enure in the role of Assistant Supervisor of Science was rather short, but extremely challenging and enjoyable. I was assigned to the regional office in Radford, Virginia. My territory was the southwestern part of the State of Virginia. It was a happy homecoming and I felt very comfortable working in the area in which I grew up. Again, life had been good to me and someone was my benefactor.

I had taught Biology, Chemistry, Physical Science, and something called General Science. Now I was in the business of supervising teachers who taught these courses. The job description was clear enough, but how does one go about performing the duties of a supervisor? I learned about this new responsibility and called it on the job training.

A whole new world of opportunity was opened up to the lad from the coal mining region of Virginia. The Virginia Department of Education served the schools from the office in Richmond and two regional offices located in Radford and in Lynchburg. I was assigned to the Radford office which was located on the campus of Radford University. William F. Young, Jr. was hired two weeks later to serve the schools in the adjacent area in the valley of Virginia. We became good friends and worked together for many years.

Responsibilities of the position included oversight of the scheduling of the NASA exhibit in schools throughout the state, coordinating activities associated with the adoption of science textbooks in the state, recommending resource materials for use in classrooms, planning conferences and workshops for teachers, and providing services to administrators.

There were many memorable moments which I enjoyed, but none more than the very first preschool conference for science teachers in the Southwest Virginia area. My colleagues in the other subject matter areas had warned me to be prepared for anything at these meetings. I expected to be introduced as the new Assistant Supervisor of Science, but not for what happened next. The teacher who was presiding over the meeting of an auditorium full of teachers made some opening remarks, introduced me and announced that I was in charge of the meeting. I do not know to this day whether it was by design, or if she had simply forgotten to inform me that I was the speaker for the day.

I enjoyed my work tremendously and was pleased that my efforts would be rendered to the schools in south western Virginia and included my old home area of Buchanan County. I learned much and came to appreciate the concern of Dr. Francis Sisson who was Director of Personnel for the city of Richmond. I was young to be supervising, organizing, and implementing the science curriculum for the state. Youth will be served, but is not always prudent. Dr. Sisson and I became friends and played golf on several occasions, but never discussed my interview for the position of Science Supervisor for the City of Richmond.

The move was very advantageous for Phyllis and me because it allowed her to transfer her work from Virginia Commonwealth University in Richmond to Radford University and complete her work for a BS degree in Business Education. She completed her degree and graduated in March and was fortunate to be selected to finish the year out as a Business Education teacher at Christiansburg High School in Montgomery County, Virginia.

Our tenure in the regional office ended with the completion of Phyllis' first full year of teaching and second year of service. The opportunity to make a lateral move into the administrative realm was the next step that I needed to take. I was offered the position of Assistant Supervisor of Secondary Education and acceptance of the new position meant a move back to Richmond. It meant

Phyllis would give up her teaching position, I would take on new responsibilities, and our first son Brian would be born in the capitol of the Confederacy.

Solomon observed in Ecclesiastes that there is a time for everything and a season for every activity under heaven. He recognized among other things that there is a time for man to toil and find satisfaction in all his toil. My tenure with the State Department of Education in Virginia was a labor of love and I didn't look upon it as a burden, but as an opportunity to learn and grow. It was a proving ground and I eagerly immersed myself in activities that made a difference in the education of young people. I did find satisfaction in my toil.

Approximately fifteen years were devoted to service in Virginia. Those years were special and exciting as they heralded the arrival of our second son, Chris. We concentrated on fulfilling our obligation to the state of Virginia and the new family. I was working full time, raising a family, and taking every opportunity to continue my formal education. The support of Phyllis was crucial to the accomplishment of my goals and objectives.

Exposure to people and experiences on a state government level gave support to the decision to move from Science Supervision to the administrative level of service. It opened up numerous opportunities to enter into related jobs in education, but we were happy to serve where we were, at least for the time.

There was one particular offer that demanded careful consideration. The offer came from Fairfax County, Virginia, one of the largest school systems in the country.

My work with them must have impressed their organization very favorably, because they offered me the position of Director of Planning at a very attractive salary. Phyllis and I were on the verge of moving to Fairfax and informed the Department that we had been offered the position and were seriously considering a move to the Washington, D.C. area.

Dr. Woodrow W. Wilkerson, who was the State Superintendent of Public Instruction, learned about the offer and asked for a conference with me before a decision was made to leave. I was still holding the position of Assistant Supervisor of Secondary Education when Numa Bradner, who was the Supervisor, resigned to take a position as Superintendent of Schools in Pulaski County, Virginia. I wanted very much to be considered for the position and if it was not available, then I could not afford to turn my back on the Fairfax position. I suspected the position was not available because I did not have experience as a principal. The only experience in that area was that of unpaid assistant principal.

Personnel matters involving the position of Supervisor and above had to be cleared through the members of the State Board of Education. Dr. Wilkerson asked what would entice me to remain with the Department. I seized the opportunity to explain my interest in the position of Supervisor of Secondary Education. I had aspired to have the opportunity to serve in that position since joining the staff in the early 1960s.

Dr. Wilkerson was a man of few words. He wanted to know if I felt I could handle the rigors associated with the position. He indicated the demands of the job were unique in that Board members and staff at that level were open prey to the media and the public at large. In fact, it would be a political appointment. My response was positive to the question and Dr. Wilkerson asked whether or not the appointment with Fairfax could be rescheduled to give them time to poll the members of the Board concerning the filling of the position. The Personnel Director of Fairfax County Schools agreed to reschedule the interview and the poll was conducted. It was my first venture into the political arena.

The Board Members gave their approval to Dr. Wilkerson to make the appointment. I was offered the position and accepted the role I had desired since joining the Virginia State Department of Education in 1961. Primary responsibilities of the position were to coordinate the services of subject area supervisors to teachers and administrative personnel in the state. Administrative duties involved working with principals and division super-intendents.

I gained the confidence of the division superintendents and principals, and before I left the Department in 1976, I knew the approximately 150 superintendents well enough to call them by their first name. The same could be said about a majority of the secondary school principals. I considered it a privilege to have worked with some of the most competent educational leaders in Virginia.

My close relationship with, and accessibility to, the school administrators in Virginia provided a solid foundation for improving the schools. I visited most of the high schools before leaving and was humbled and gratified when a large majority of the superintendents and many of the principals expressed in person and in writing their regrets when I announced my resignation to take a position with the Southern Association of Colleges and Schools in Atlanta, Georgia.

Before leaving Virginia and the Department, a number of significant developments came to fruition under my supervision. The first attempts at data processing of reports for the state accreditation program paved the way from clumsy trial and error technology to unbelievable strides in school improvement supported by sophisticated technology that is state of the art. I do not take credit for the development of this process, but it happened on my watch. A number of people were involved, but a large part of the work was directed by Dr. Charles Clear who was Director of Research for the Department.

I directed the revision of the standards for accrediting schools and streamlined the State's school evaluation process. I was also a part of the effort to write Standards of Quality for schools and assigned the first black man, Gilbert Mays, to coordinate the self-study and peer review of a predominately white school. There were a few tense moments, but strong leadership from the principal, from Gilbert Mays and support from the faculty and parents carried the day.

Workshops were developed and refined for involving teachers, administrators, and supervisors to improve the evaluation and accreditation program for schools in Virginia. Credit again goes to a competent and knowledgeeable staff that worked tirelessly to train thousands of teachers and administrators.

One of the responsibilities of the Supervisor of Secondary Education was to serve as Executive Secretary to the Virginia State Committee of the Southern Association of Colleges and Schools. SACS was one of six regional accrediting organizations that provided organized, systematic school improvement through accreditation. SACS served eleven states from Virginia south through Florida and west through Texas. It also accredited the American Schools in the Latin Republics. It was through this activity that I became involved in the international arena and was elected to the position of Chairman of the Commission on Secondary and Middle Schools of the Association. This responsibility was in addition to the regular duties as Supervisor of Secondary Education for the State Department of Education. Working with the Superintendent and the State Board of Education was certainly different. It was, by no means, a nine-to-five job. I was on call to the Superintendent and the Board at all times. However, it was where I wanted to be.

Words that reached the media and the public had to be carefully chosen and even then the questions posed by the media elicited responses that sounded different from what I thought I had said. I knew the reason for the Superintendent's earlier question. More times than not staff members were expected to take responsibility for reports to the media or the Board that were considered to be "in process."

For example, my staff and I completed a report on the accreditation status of schools which indicated that a number of schools would be placed on the list with a probation status. Keep in mind this report was presented with the media listening to every word. That report was presented in October, and was considered by the Board at each monthly meeting until it was finally accepted at the May meeting. The media had a field day and my phone was ringing constantly. Talk about choosing words carefully! There was never a dull moment. Sensationalism was what they were after and any slip of the tongue could mean reprimand or dismissal for the staff member.

BEYOND THE HORIZON: TO EXPLORE NEW WORLDS

T he unpaid position of Chairman of the Commission of Secondary Schools of SACS opened new vistas. I coordinated the duties of Supervisor of Secondary Education for the State Department of Education, the job I was paid to perform, and fulfilled the responsibilities of the Chair of the Commission of SACS which was a unpaid position. The dual responsibilities were compatible and ultimately led to my appointment to serve in a fulltime position with SACS. After fifteen years of service to the state of Virginia in that dual role, I was offered and accepted the position of Associate Executive Director for the Commission on Secondary Schools of SACS.

The title carried with it the awesome responsibility to direct and coordinate the activities of eleven State Committees and organize and direct the work of the central office staff in Atlanta. I was appointed Executive Director of the Commission in 1995. As Executive Director, I was responsible for serving as CEO and Executive Director of the Association on an alternating basis with Dr. James Rogers of the Commission on Colleges and Dr. John Davis of the Commission on Elementary and Middle Schools. My tenure with SACS spanned more than a quarter century.

School improvement through accreditation began in the late 1800s for stateside institutions and was followed by American/International Schools in the early 1900s. While I served as Executive Director, I was privileged to be elected to serve on the Board of Directors of the National Study of School Evaluation (NSSE). I served on that organization for fifteen years and as its Chair for eleven years. NSSE was the research arm of the six regional accrediting associations and was responsible for developing the evaluative criteria and resource materials for use in the evaluation and accreditation process in schools in the United States and abroad. *How ironic*, I thought. The publication was the one I had been perusing while waiting in Dr. Thompson's office to be interviewed for the position with the State Department of Education. Another near miss that could have sent my career spinning had I not made the decision to choose the path less travelled.

The National Study of School Evaluation was formed in the 1940s and consisted of representatives from the six regional accrediting associations. The Board of Directors was a large group of people who served as the research arm of the regionals. It became an unwieldy organization and at times was ineffective. The makeup of the Board depended on the number of schools that were accredited by each regional. There were five members from the Southern Association, five from North Central, four from Middle States, three from Northwest, three from New England, and three from Western. The membership fluctuated as the sales of the *Evaluative Criteria* and support materials increased or decreased. The regionals nominated their representatives to be on the Board who were dutifully elected by the total Board.

My second meeting as a Board member was in Hawaii. What a beautiful place to hold a meeting. It was a bittersweet time for me in that John Vaughn of the North Central Association was chair of NSSE and became ill and could not attend the meeting. John knew that it was just a matter of time and he asked if I would fill out his term. Of course I would, but it would be with a heavy heart. I went to the Hawaii meeting and did not expect to have any problems with what had transpired. Was I ever in for a surprise! It became apparent that the New England Association clearly believed that one of their own, Robert O'Donnell, should be the next Chair of NSSE. I found myself in the middle of a power struggle, and had only wanted to do a favor to a dying friend. It was, to say the least, an interesting turn of events.

I became more aware that the majority of the Board members were not as opposed to Bob O'Donnell as Chair as they were with the New England Association and the power behind that organization. Approval of the Board was necessary to fill an expired term and the item found its way to the agenda for the last day of the meeting. This gave plenty of time for campaigning and there was an abundance of discussion both in the open and behind closed doors.

Thankfully, the last day of the meeting was called to order and the issue was before the board. Several speeches were delivered and a secret ballot was used three times with the final vote being a show of hands. The results did not vary and I was elected Chair of the NSSE.

As expected, the following year was an election year, and the issue was on the agenda. The campaign speeches were as vocal as before and the results were also the same. I went on to serve eleven years as Chair. I was very much saddened because Bob O'Donnell was a very good friend and the relationship was never the same. He was always agreeable but politely cool. Sometimes decisions bring consequences that are unpleasant; if we could live life over, we'd never be certain that taking the other path would not have been preferred.

The National Study was effective for many years, but the needs of schools for more relevant criteria and new approaches became more and more critical. The decline in the use of materials and services led to the takeover of the Study by the Southern Association in the mid 1990s. It was absorbed into the new organization called AdvancED which is the parent organization of the North Central Association, Southern Association and the National Study.

The NSSE provided materials and services for more than a half century to guide the evaluation/accreditation for school improvement, but it was going the route of the dinosaur, and more and more the question was, "Is that all there is?" NSSE was absorbed into AdvancED to play a different role in the school improvement process.

I enjoyed the work immensely and it was never boring. It was not unusual to be conducting a workshop on school improvement in Jackson, Mississippi one day and board a plane the next day to visit schools in Sao Paulo, Brazil or La Paz, Bolivia. Activities on the international level provided some unique and interesting experiences. It was also not out of the ordinary to be dining with heads of state and ambassadors one day, and sampling the culinary delights of a wild beast that had been cooked for hours in the ground the next day.

Experiencing different cultures up close and personal was a perk that was worth its weight in gold. I learned to appreciate the extra caution to avoid the embarrassment of an improper gesture or an inappropriate phrase. It was always interesting to decide how to avoid insulting the host or hostess while managing to eat food that would not cause infestation of some exotic germ or virus.

The opportunity to ride up the side of a live volcano in Nicaragua and climb carefully over the edge to see the red hot boiling lava was a once in a lifetime experience. Then there was the day long train ride from Cuzco into the interior of Peru to climb 8,000 feet by bus to experience the wonder of Machu Picchu. A trip to the 38th parallel of the Demilitarized Zone (DMZ) where I stood and gazed at the

North Korean soldiers staring back from less than fifty yards away, gave silent testimony to the serious and sinister nature of the duty of the U.S. troops who keep vigil at these perilous outposts. Reason enough to assure that quality educational programs were available to the troops on the front line.

Education is truly the key that unlocks the doors to the good, the bad and the ugly of our world. My work not only took me to all fifty states except North and South Dakota, but also to many interesting and exotic places in the world. I saw firsthand the abject poverty of Haiti, the teeming masses of Hong Kong and Korea, the beauty and tranquility of Vienna, the old world charm and wonder of Italy, the pomp and ceremony of England, and the frustration of air travel in Japan. My work with school improvement through accreditation also took us to virtually every country of South America, Central America, Mexico and the Islands of the Caribbean.

One of the things I treasured most about the many years of service in education was the privilege to work with the most dedicated, knowledgeable and distinguished people in the world. That privilege had its origin in the classrooms at Grundy High School and reached throughout the world. A positive side effect of this effort to record significant events that impacted my life and those around me, is that I have been able to recall events and experiences that I thought had been lost forever. I cherished all these memories and the wonderful people with whom I had the opportunity to serve. Many of their names are listed in the appendix in the back of this book.

Responsibilities of the Director of the Commission on Secondary Schools of the Southern Association of Colleges and Schools included the evaluation and accreditation of schools as an option. To gain accreditation status, the schools were required to conduct a self-study and invite a peer review team to validate the school's findings and their plans for improving the school. The peer review teams were composed of educators from other American Schools and teachers and administrators from the States.

The work of peer review teams was intense and was completed in three or four days. Teams were small in number so it was imperative they stay well during the visit. Team members were trained and underwent orientation prior to the on-site visit. An important part of the orientation included some dos and don'ts such as "don't drink the water," and "don't eat raw fruits and vegetables" that had not been treated.

Every effort was made to inform team members of the folly of eating and drinking indiscriminately to avoid becoming ill. The cautions were important because the team could not accomplish their purpose if they were sick. There were those people who had cast iron stomachs and never became ill and there were those who could just think about it and become ill. Giving in to the temptation to enjoy a green salad or a bright red strawberry could be a very bad decision. Fortunately, the hosts in the schools were cognizant of the potential problem, and prepared food accordingly.

Some team members took precautions and still became ill. Maybe it was a case of think you are ill and you will be.

It could have been that bottled water or a soft drink was poured over ice cubes frozen from tap water. I came to enjoy warm sodas and "agua con gas" (water with bubbles or carbonated water) and never became ill in all my travels overseas.

The following vignette is included for good friend John Davis. John was the Executive Director of the Commission on Elementary and Middle Schools of SACS. He indicated a desire to be on one of the teams to visit one of the overseas schools. He was assigned to a team, informed of the dos and don'ts, properly trained, and sent on his way.

The visiting team finished its work and returned home. I was anxious to hear from John about his experience and whether or not he enjoyed the trip. He assured me that it was a once in a lifetime opportunity and he made not one, but two visits: his first and his last. It was a surprise that he did not care to be part of another team. When asked why he would not be interested, he admitted that he had become ill near the end of the visit. When he was asked whether he had followed the instructions, he assured me that he had. He had brushed his teeth in bottled water and drank only the water in the lobby that came from a large bottle of water. After drinking water from the bottle of water in the lobby, he had taken a walk. He was surprised to see a hotel employee filling one of the large bottles from the outside spigot. It was bottled water, but the source was not from a safe reservoir. He who deviates from the rules, even if it appears to be safe, must be wary or Montezuma will exact his revenge.

Peer Review Team Visits Overseas School

YOUR CHOICE MAY CHANGE
THE WORLD

E fforts to improve schools began in the nineteenth century were expanded to involve state and regional efforts, and spread to include schools worldwide. School improvement through accreditation was uniquely American, non-governmental, optional, and researched based. It has become the premiere process by which schools are recognized the world over.

American/International Schools in the Latin Republics sought recognition and approval from the Southern Association as early as 1930 when the American School of Mexico pursued and gained accredited status. From that beginning, the program grew and by the year 2000 more than one hundred schools were accredited or in candidate status for accreditation from virtually every country in Mexico, Central America, South America, and the Islands of the Caribbean. The other five regionals expanded the program to include other parts of the world. Since 2001 reorganization and expansion of the school improvement through accreditation has opened exciting new possibilities for educational institutions all over the world including China; programs to improve schools in the U.S. and abroad have been accomplished largely through voluntary efforts. Thousands of schools and millions of teachers, parents and students have involved themselves in school self- studies since the inception of the program. There are thousands of peer review teams who donate their time to help schools gain and maintain their accredited status. The program works because dedicated people give their time and support to the effort. People like Dr. Gurney Chambers, Frank Anderson, Dr. Burton Fox, and others like them, believed fervently in the school improvement process and volunteered their time to help schools to improve.

I followed the men who blazed the trail for accreditation in the South and in the Latin Republics. The work of improving schools through self-study and peer review was unique to the United States. The schools that committed to improvement through this process were recognized by receiving accreditation. The pioneers who organized and led the movement were truly people dedicated to helping schools. They were employed by educational institutions, but volunteered their time to help the new program to succeed. It began in the late nineteenth century and continues to thrive. Paid staff was added slowly when it became evident that growth made it necessary to give full-time direction and guidance to a movement that was destined to flourish.

The changing of the guard came about when I retired on December 31, 2001, and the organization which had been a stalwart in school improvement and accreditation expanded to include schools from all over the world. The giants who had developed the process by which schools could commit themselves to school improvement and be recognized through accreditation for their efforts, had laid a sound foundation on which a new era could grow and flourish. Accreditation was a part of a larger movement that was on the brink of an exciting thrust that would change the world.

THE SEARCH FOR QUALITY

T he program of regional accreditation began in the late 1880's and its unique program of self-evaluation and peer review to bring about school improvement has grown steadily over the years. It was like the "Good Housekeeping" seal of approval. It was also attractive because it did not attempt to dictate what a school had to be, but if it desired to be counted with the best educational institutions, then accreditation through the self-evaluation, peer review process and subjecting themselves to standards of quality was a given.

People often criticized the process, but were hesitant to allow schools to lose their accreditation. While the large majority of the stakeholders understood the importance of subjecting their schools to standards of quality, and of the necessity of committing to an organized systematic, program for school improvement, there were those who ignored the standards and lost their accreditation. The loss of accreditation usually raised a red flag and indicated serious problems in the schools. When publicity revealed the inability of a school to meet standards and subsequently be cited for lack of commitment to a systematic approach to school improvement, several consequences were evident. Acceptance of credit earned in an unaccredited school becomes a problem, transfer of credit also becomes a problem, and business and industry are reluctant to locate in an area where schools are not accredited, just to mention a few repercussions and consequences. Even more important was the lack of a concerted effort to be working to provide a quality educational program for students.

Many people labored to perfect the process and there is no way to properly recognize and thank them all, but I would be remiss if I did not give some recognition for some of those who went the extra mile to make it work. The stalwarts who developed and nurtured the program provide the shoulders on which all others stand, Dr. Raymond G. Wilson, Dr. W. R. "Dub" Goodson, and Dr. Joseph M. Johnston. I consider myself fortunate to have had the privilege to work side by side with these unique individuals.

There were times when I and two secretaries occupied the office in Atlanta. It was then that the true loyalty and support of Mrs. Ione Winn was most valuable. She was a beacon as the staff on Peachtree Street sought to provide service to schools through state committees. State committees coordinated the evaluation and accreditation activities with guidance and direction from the staff. Travel was their middle name and though it was difficult, my staff and I endured and enjoyed the rigors of directing the regional accreditation program in the South.

Charles Fugitt joined the staff in Atlanta and was immersed in the efforts to computerize annual reports. Neither he nor I knew much about data processing so the decision was made to outsource the processing of annual reports to the state of Texas through the Texas State Committee. Charlie took the lead and the Age of Aquarius was upon us. It cost an arm and a leg, but it was a beginning. It became more expensive and the problems mounted. I decided enough was enough and the process was moved to the Atlanta office. It was a small step for accreditation, and one that proved to be a giant move forward. The staff grew, and the work demanded more staff and more resources. Mont Bush was added to the staff to provide support for schools and school systems.

Mark Elgart was recruited to provide some leadership to the middle/junior high school program. As it turned out, his knowledge of technology was far more valuable and it helped the SACS Commission on Secondary and Middle Schools to set the stage for the evolution of an exciting new corporate organization to spread the concept of school improvement over the world. And the rest of the story is yet to be told.

Mark is the current President and CEO of AdvancED and directs the program for accreditation of all schools including the American/International institutions. He succeeded me as Executive Director of SACS, Commission on Secondary and Middle Schools to become the fifth person to hold that position since its inception. In five short years, Mark led the restructuring of the organization as it evolved into a worldwide effort to improve schools.

Accreditation of schools is still accomplished through the work of SACS for the schools in the eleven Southern state region and the schools in the twenty-state region of the North Central Association. Myriad materials and resources have been developed to assist schools as they seek to improve and be recognized as quality institutions. AdvancED is the corporate structure which promotes accreditation and provides the resources, materials and structure to make school improvement a reality.

Dedicated people built a strong foundation for school improvement and they continue to stress the value of good schools and quality educational institutions for youngsters all over the world. No one has done more for school improvement, nor has anyone been more dedicated to the cause of school improvement than Dr. Ray Bruce. His work with teachers and administrators in Georgia and the U.S. is unparalleled, and he has worked with virtually every American /International School in the Latin Republics. Ray was like an unpaid staff member of the Commission, and he often said that the opportunity to work with the overseas schools was all the pay he wanted.

My many years of service to education were extraordinarily fulfilling and satisfying, principally because it was an opportunity to help schools to improve and in so doing helped children all over the world. It provided the venue to fulfill dreams and reach for the stars. The help and support from countless individuals made it possible to be a part of many wonderful experiences that would not have happened otherwise. Caring people were always there and that made all the difference.

The willingness to provide and, in some cases, to give themselves totally to this concept to improve schools has made it the premiere process for recognizing educational quality the world over. I was much indebted to be a part of this effort and count myself fortunate to work with so many top professionals in education. How can one individual be so fortunate? A very special place in my heart is reserved for the staff in Atlanta who made me look good through their dedicated and competent work. Whatever accolades have been showered on me belong to Mrs. Ione Winn, Mark Elgart, Joan Rohrbach, Charles Fugitt, Mont Bush, Ray Bruce and all the central office personnel. Their efforts paved the way for hundreds of dedicated people to make invaluable contributions to the improvement of education all over the world.

The friends and colleagues I was fortunate to work with were a special group of people. I accepted recognition from several groups and organizations, but must quickly pass the praise to the many people who deserved the honor. I was humbled to accept induction into the Hall of Fame of the Association for the Advancement of International Education and to serve as Agent for the Association of American Schools in South America and the Tri-Association of American Schools in Central America,

Mexico, and the Islands of the Caribbean. A certificate of appreciation was presented to me by the U.S. Department of State for work with overseas schools and was given the title of Executive Director Emeritus when I retired after forty-five years of service in education.

I was also pleased to receive the King College Distinguished Alumnus Award for 2005. A scholarship was established in my honor to be awarded to deserving individuals for outstanding contributions to education. The awards are listed on behalf of the many people whose efforts made them possible. If I am to be recognized for anything, it should be for having the knowledge and insight to recognize and utilize people for the talents they possess.

It is impossible to recognize all who have been involved since the program of evaluation and accreditation was started in the late 1880s. There have been literally millions of people involved in this process either as students, parents, teachers, administrators, college personnel, and members of the lay public. Education touches everyone and each individual is changed in one way or another. The effects of all these changes have resulted in positive improvement which is trending on an upward scale. Everything in the name of education is not successful, but it is far and above what could be expected if the effort to improve was simply left to chance. Thank goodness there have been and will continue to be individuals and groups of people who dedicate their lives to make education a high priority and consequently, make the world a better place to live.

It was my privilege to work with many dedicated individuals who have spent their lives making life better through education. There is a group I worked with that had its origin in the John F. Kennedy administration and continues to be much involved with the education of children who are in the American/International schools all over the world. The Office of Overseas Schools of the U.S. Department of State was the organization charged with the care and well-being of these students in all parts of the world. Dr. Ernest N. Mannino was appointed to serve as Director of the new Department by President Kennedy and he served in that capacity until he retired. Dr. Keith Miller was appointed to succeed Dr. Mannino and he currently serves in that position. It was a privilege for me to work with Dr. Mannino and Dr. Miller and other members of the staff. I was especially proud to work with Dr. Salvatorie Rinaldi as a friend and colleague as we travelled the world seeking to provide help and assistance to U.S. and International Schools Abroad.

State Department Dinner

Colin Powell welcomes members of the Overseas Schools
Advisory Council in the Department of the State.

A FINAL WORD

This project began innocently enough and once the memories started they became a constant flow with each event and experience struggling to be included. Efforts to stay focused and to limit the recollection of events and experiences to those that supported the stated purpose were at the mercy of an overflowing dam of pent up memories. Then there were the times that I had to step back and ask myself "What if...?" What if my mother and I had not taken time to dream? What if a guardian angel had not been around to protect an innocent and sometimes foolish youngster? What if there had not been a caring principal, a Christian oriented college community, a college president who would not take "I can't" as an alternative, a loving and supportive family, someone or something to preserve a one second victory, and myriad other crossroads decisions? However, life is what it is and we are what we are because we have experienced it.

All of the events and experiences had consequences and life changing implications that combined to sculpt my personality. The lives of those who were touched by me were hopefully better for having had the experience as was I for having had the privilege of touching their lives.

Do we dare reach for the stars? We did; along the way some of our dreams became reality. We have experienced life and have been changed. We are what we are as a result of those experiences and our responses to them. We have encountered a number of crossroads and we chose the path less travelled and it has made all the difference. Whether we became all we could be is for each individual to decide. Perhaps those who follow will be guided by what they have observed from those of us who have gone before.

The final word? The final word has not yet been uttered.

Dreams for a better tomorrow rest with the children whose lives have been entrusted for those of us who came to the mountain, climbed the mountain, and dared to pursue the dream and reach for the stars. Dare to care; dare to be different; dare to believe that the road less travelled can be that which makes a difference, dare to reach for the impossible- dream the unreachable star. The unlikely journey has been an adventure that I will never forget.

APPENDIX

I mprovement of schools through evaluation/ accreditation is effective because those individuals who were involved contributed time and effort to make it work. It is impossible to list everyone; this appendix is representative of the diversity of those who dared to make a difference.

National Study of School Evaluation (NSSE)

Southern Association of Colleges and Schools
Central Staff

Aho, Dr. Frederick – Executive Director, Middle States Association for Colleges and Schools, Pennsylvania

Anderson, Frank – Overseas Director, Venezuela

Baker, Dr. Stephen – Executive Director, Southern Association of Colleges and Schools, Georgia

Bennett, Dr. Pamela-Gray – Southern Association of Colleges and Schools and New England Association of Colleges and Schools, Massachusetts

Bentz, Dr. Carlton – Associate Director, Office of Overseas Schools, Washington, D.C.

Besteiro, Raul – Superintendent, Texas

Bradner, Numa – Executive Director for Commission of Secondary Schools, State Department of Education, Virginia

Bradley, Dr. Richard – Director, New England Association of Colleges and Schools, Massachusetts

Broman, Dr. Forrest – Overseas Consultant, Massachusetts

Brown, Dr. Gilbert – Overseas Director, Rio de Janeiro, Brazil

Brown, Dr. Mark – Professor, University of Kentucky, Lexington, Kentucky

Brunner, Dr. Carolyn – Professor, Buffalo State University, Buffalo, New York

Bryan, Dr. Sandy – Professor, Kennesaw State University, Kennesaw, Georgia

Campbell, Sister Camille Anne – Superintendent, Louisiana

Caywood, John – Principal, Virginia

Chambers, Dr. Gurney – Professor, University of Western Carolina, Culawhee, North Carolina

Clear, Dr. Charles – Director of Research, State Department of Education, Richmond, Virginia

Cox, Dr. John Ed – Director of State Committee, State Department of Education, Tennessee

Crocker, Dr. William – Superintendent, Alabama

Cummings, Dr. Jay – Professor, Texas

Davis, Dr. John M. – Director of Elementary Education, Southern Association of Colleges and Schools, Atlanta, Georgia

Delaney, Dr. Joseph – Principal, North Carolina

Delmon, Dr. Jack – Overseas Director

Fitzpatrick, Dr. Kathleen – Director, National Study of School Evaluation, Illinois

Fox, Dr. Burton – Director, Inter Regional Center, Alabama

Fulmer, Dr. Robert – State Director, State Department of Education, South Carolina

Fuccillo, Dr. Lou – Education Consultant, Massachusetts

Graham, Dr. James –Superintendent, Virginia

Gillies, Dr. Warna – Professor, Bowie State University, Bowie, Maryland

Gremillion, Dr. Burton – Professor, Louisiana State University, Louisiana

Greer, Dr. John – Professor, Georgia State University, Atlanta, Georgia

Gose, Dr. Kenneth – Executive Director, North Central Association of Colleges and Schools, Arizona

Hamic, Buddy – School Administrator, Louisiana

Hunt, Dr. Nile – State Director, State Department of Education, North Carolina

Harp, Lauree – Treasurer/Secretary, National Study of School Evaluation, Illinois

Haught, Dr. Donald – Executive Director, Western Association of Colleges and Schools, California

Jewell, Dr. Robert – Executive Director of the State Committee, State Department of Education, Virginia

Jernberg, Dr. Peter – School Administrator, Mississippi

Johnson, Dr. William – Professor, University of Central Florida, Orlando, Florida

Johnson, Dr. H. F. – Superintendent, Georgia

Keller, Dr. Jeffery – Overseas Director, Mexico

Klumpp, Dr. Dennis – Overseas Director, Paraguay

Kemp, Dr. John – Professor, University of Illinois, Champaign, Illinois

Lawrence, Dr. Jimmie – School Superintendent, Alabama

Lee, Dr. Tennent – Professor, University of Alabama, Alabama

Lamb, Dr. Elsa – Overseas Director, Association for Advancement in International Education

Magugan, Dr. Vincent – Associate Director of the Office of Overseas Schools, United States Government, Washington, D.C.

Maidment, Dr. Robert – Professor, William and Mary College, Williamsburg, Virginia

Mannino, Dr. Ernie – Director of the Office of Overseas Schools, United States Government, Washington, D.C.

Marino, Dr. Ronald – School Administrator, Illinois

Manlove, Dr. Donald – Executive Director, National Study of School Evaluation, Indiana

Manly, Dr. Theron – Professor, University of Southern Mississippi, Hattiesburg, Mississippi

Meade, John – Principal, Virginia

Merril, Wallace – Supervisor of Secondary Education, State Department of Education, Mississippi

Miller, Dr. Keith – Director of the Office of Overseas Schools, United States Government, Washington, D.C.

Morris, Dr. James – Overseas Director, Florida

Mosely, Dr. James – Professor, University of Alabama, Tuscaloosa, Alabama

Orr, Dr. Paul – Professor, University of Alabama, Tuscaloosa, Alabama

Pace, Dr. Vernon – National Study of School Evaluation, University of Indiana, Bloomington, Indiana

Pasquale, Dr. Frederick – Educational Consultant, California

Patterson, Dr. Tom – Principal, Texas

Penland, Dr. Herm – Overseas Director, La Paz, Bolivia

Philips, Dr. Kent – Director of Secondary Education, State Department of Education, South Carolina

Pierce, Dr. Robin – Superintendent, Tennessee

Rinaldi, Dr. Salvatore – Associate Director of Office for Overseas Schools, United States Government, Washington, D.C.

Robinson, Capt. Dale – Educational Administrator, Florida

Richardson, Dr. Tom – General Motors Youth Education, Alabama

Redmon, Dr. Tom – Consultant, Georgia

Rose, Dr. Jack – Superintendent, Kentucky

Ruffin, Durrell – Director of Elementary Commission, Southern Association of Colleges and Schools, Georgia

Sams, Dr. Everett – Professor, Middle Tennessee University, Murfreesboro, Tennessee

Sanchez, Dr. Mary – Overseas Director, Quito, Ecuador

Scotti, Dr. William – Overseas Director, United States Government, Washington, D.C.

Selitzer, Dr. Jerry – Overseas Director, Mexico

Shufflebarger, Dr. Emmett – Director of Secondary Commission, State Department of Education, Virginia

Smith, Dr. Connie – Director of Secondary Education, State Department of Education, Tennessee

Smith, Dr. Leland – Professor, University of Kentucky, Lexington, Kentucky

Steadman, Dr. David – Executive Director, Northwest Association of Schools and Colleges, Idaho

Stanford, Dr. Ronnie – Professor, University of Alabama, Tuscaloosa, Alabama

Storer, Dr. Robert –Superintendent, Kentucky

Takcas, Dr. George – Overseas Director, Brazil

Thomas, Dr. Albert – Superintendent, Texas

Tucker, John – Superintendent, North Carolina

Tully, Dr David – Overseas Director, Sao Paulo, Brazil

Weaver, Dr. Andy – Professor, Auburn University, Auburn, Alabama

Winstead, Dr. Frank – Consultant, Texas

Wilkerson, Dr. Woodrow – State Superintendent, Virginia

Walker, Dr. Joe – Overseas Director, Venezuela

Williams, Dr. Irvin – Executive Director of the State Committee, State Department of Education, Richmond, Virginia

Wilson, Dr. Hugh – School Superintendent, Mississippi

DeVaughn, Dr. Everette – Professor, Georgia State University, Atlanta, Georgia

Young, Dr. William F. – Executive Director of the State Committee, State Department of Education, Virginia

BIBLIOGRAPHY

Hurley, Sam, and Judge Willis Staton. *A Colorful Career of a Miraculous Mountaineer: A Glimpse into the Life of a Remarkable Character.* Pikeville, KY: 1943.

Life Application Bible: New International Version. Grand Rapids, MI: Zondervan, 1991.